Sooo...
How was your day?

BRENDA HAMMON

Copyright ©2021 Brenda Hammon

Art Cover: Laurel Hawkswell

ISBN: 978-1-953806-43-7

Printed in Canada, all rights reserved. No part of this book may be used in any way or reproduced in any manner including mechanical, photographic or electronic process, or in the form of phonographic recording; nor may it be stored in a retrieval system, transmitted, or otherwise copied for public or private use without the written permission of the Author or Publisher.

Note to the reader: This book is not intended to dispense psychological or therapeutic advice. The information is provided for educational and inspirational and humorous purposes only. In the event, you use any of the information in this book for yourself, which is your constitutional right, the author and publisher assumes no responsibility for your actions. Although the Author, Participants and Publisher has made every effort to ensure that the information in this book was correct at press time, the Author, Participants and Publisher does not assume and hereby declaims any liability to any party for any loss, damage, or disruption by errors or omission, whether such error and omission result from negligence, accidents, or any other cause.

Disclaimer: This book is intend for personal use.

Story 13 Photo: Source: Story photo courtesy: Cat Ballou- Photo of Lee Marvin in the 1965 movie.

Some photos are free images from pixel. Personal photos cannot be reproduced or copied in any manner from this book.

Acknowledgements

Thank you to everyone who has been in my life,
without you most of these stories would not have been.
Laurel Hawkswell for the cover art illustrations.
Cathy Cassie for doing the first round of edits on each story.
Bud Portwood for his constant support in my endeavours.

Foreword

Growing up in small-town Canada meant we made our fun. Hot summer days were for hiking, riding bareback through the paths, but mostly, hot summer days were for swimming in the river while keeping watch for rattlesnakes, which also enjoyed taking a dip from time to time.

And there was the daydreaming of far-off adventures from stories I had read. I loved the stories that were true to life and funny. Stories that made me laugh out loud and cheer for the protagonist. In those stories, I saw bits of myself. No matter the age, we are all yearning to connect or make sense of life.

And reminded as Helen Keller said, "Life is either a daring adventure or nothing."

When asked to write the forward for this book of life and hilarity, I found myself remembering my many shenanigans and laughing. Each of these stories offers lessons and laughter.

Brenda's enthusiasm for life is like nothing I have ever known or seen before.

As a writer and international speaker, I have worked with some of the most amazing people. Brenda Hammon is such a person. Her sense of humor, which causes belly laughs and happy tears - is rare and instantly contagious.

Brenda lives every moment at high speed and yet is fully present. Her life is full of moments, milestones, and at times, mishaps, and her true stories are something you can not make up. Brenda's take on life revolves around fun and laughter, and she doesn't ever take herself too seriously.

If you ever have the privilege of meeting Brenda, it won't be long before you hear her ask, "How hard can it be?"

In this book, you will find stories of real-life hilarity and stories that may inspire you to write a thing or two down of your own because life is full of moments, milestones, and at times mishaps.

Jo Dibblee 2021
Author of Frock Off; Living Undisguised

Introduction

Life takes us down many roads, some roads we enjoy, and some we don't. How we look at life also affects how we handle life. The stories in this book, the challenges of life and the difficulties I encountered I looked at with a slight tweak or tilt of my head. Things looked different, how I felt about myself looked different.

I challenge you to look at your own life experiences with a tweak or tilt of your head and see what marvelous new insights you will gain from your own life experiences.

For everything thing in life there is an opposite waiting to be seen; ying and yang, up and down, positive and negative. Not everything is so black and white.

Table of Contents

1. Flying High! 9
2. Not Funny! 15
3. Are these for real? 19
4. Where did everyone go? 25
5. The Wild Things. 29
6. Are We Nuts? 35
7. If I had a Hammer 39
8. A Willy of Sorts 43
9. Au Naturelle. 47
10. To pee or not to pee, that is the question! 53
11. Free Falling! 57
12. Which Way is Up? 65
13. What do You Mean, I'm not straight? 69
14. Driving the Lines? 75
15. Some days, I wonder! 79
16. The Irish Dance 87
17. Are you Insane? 95

18. How was your night? ...101
19. The Jesus Pillow ... 105
20. Wonder Womannnn? ...111
21. Am I build weird? ...117
22. I am not helpless, I can do it! ... 123
23. You're Kidding Right?... 129
24. Draggin Behind... 135
25. What the hell was I thinking? ...141
26. What does self-care have to do with it? ... 147
27. Disney World or Bust ...151
28. My, what lovely ears you have! ... 157
29. Apples and Trees ... 163
30. Who on earth would Willingly to do this? ...171
31. How hard can it be? Dam hard. ... 175
32. Finding the Mini Cooper ...181
33. The Taco of Sorts!... 189
34. Double or Nothing!... 193
35. Mario Reborn, NOT!... 199
36. Splish, Splash and Flash... 203
37. Seriously! ... 213
38. Are you my Human?... 217
39. Exercise is overrated, if you almost die doing it!... 223
40. No good deed goes unpunished!... 227
A Woman with a Purpose – Brenda Hammon... 233

Story 1

Flying High!
1989-2012

Arion was the love of my life.

Standing 16.2 hands high, he was a dark bay Anglo Trakhener gelding with big soft liquid eyes and the softest muzzle around! I don't think I will ever have another horse like him: I had raised him from a foal, and we had a connection, an understanding that he owned me; I did not own him! He was truly unique.

Arion helped me through so many hurdles in my life, and I in turn helped him through all the health crises he had in his life. We had a deep connection, a love of sorts, the kind that's only available to those who truly understand each other. I would give my life to keep him safe, and unfortunately it nearly came to that. (That story you will find in my book called *"I Am, Breaking Down the Walls of Silence."* However this story is a happy one, a tale of two strong-minded individuals!)

Arion and I developed a good working-system over time that called for gentle cues and mutual respect. Therefore, he was very particular about other riders on his back. Many times my trainers found themselves punted to the ground after using a crop on him. Even after my warnings about not whipping him, they didn't always listen and found themselves airborne! If Arion thought that he was doing what you asked of him, he was fine with taking commands. On the other hand, if you over-corrected him with a whip, he became offended, and you were tossed to the ground! In the end, none of my dressage trainers would ride him.

Arion was a handful, with a strong personality to match: we were well suited for each other!!

Dressage was Arion's favourite thing to do! Now most people would much rather do show-jumping with their horses, but Arion *detested the jumps!* Even though he was very talented at jumping, it always felt like I was taking my life in my hands when we did, for his displeasure was clearly evident! You see, as he was going over the hated jumps, he would somehow manage to flip his tail up over his back and slap me in the face, while at the same time almost propelling me "over the handlebars" if I wasn't paying close attention! (I might add: this happened a lot at first, but as we grew together we eventually came to an understanding of sorts.)

As time went on, I realized that as I was getting older, my body no longer bounced well when Arion tossed me! Now it was more like a cow-patty hitting the ground, exploding everywhere. It was taking longer to peel myself out of the dirt, kicking the soil back over the huge divot my not-so-graceful landing created. Finally, older and wiser, the day came when I decided to quit torturing myself: I would dedicate my riding days solely to Dressage!

I could almost hear Arion laughing at that, saying, "Finally she gets it!"

One May long-weekend, we were in Killarney, near Edmonton for a two-day Dressage competition.

The morning air was warm and crisp, and I was hoping for beautiful May weather in spite of my opposite experiences of the past.

My first ride would be first thing in the morning, and I was scheduled to be the last rider of the weekend. The Alberta Equestrian Federation (AEF) and the Canadian Dressage (CDC) had made several amendments to the rules, so now amateur riders like me could ride their tests with professionals. Thus I would have nine tests to get it right. Nine tests!

My good friend Patti and I had just finished polishing-up Arion for his first test. It is extremely difficult to keep a dark bay horse clean in the sand arenas but we were certainly hard at it!

Just as we were about to enter the warm-up arena, my cellphone rang! It was my estranged husband calling to complain that his truck would not start! (Seriously Dude?!) I am not sure what he expected me to do about it! Not only am I not a mechanic, but he was five hundred miles away in the bush... maybe I was supposed to wave my friggin' magic wand to start his truck! Here I was, ready to be tested with my horse, trying hard to focus on the job at hand but the more he bitched at me the more agitated I was getting. Finally he hung up and I could get back to the task before me, but before I could get up on Arion, my phone rang again.

This time it was a co-worker named Bud. He called to wish me luck and to "knock 'em dead!" As I thanked him for the call, my anxiety began to dissipate! Arion, in the meantime, was looking at me as if to say, "Would you HURRY UP? I am raring to go!!"

I can safely admit that both of us fed off of each other's excitement, and at that moment we were charging each other with high-octane explosive fuel! The minute I sat on his back, Arion was off like a rocket, ready to eat up the arena! He was proudly showing off his moves and strutting his stuff!

Suddenly, we were alongside a show-jump setup. Arion *hated* those dreadful jumps, so now he was shying away, doing the world's best half-pass with cadence to spare, glaring at it with eyes bugged out, and snorting like a fire-breathing dragon! Once we were past this apparently big scary object of terror, we proceeded around the arena with so much impulsion it was like riding a time bomb! Arion's blood was up now and he refused to settle down. I felt like a pimple sitting on top of a volcano that was ready to burst at the seams! Unfortunately, there were still more of those damned jumps set up, and Arion was starting to lose his mind! He was not much into thinking or paying any attention to any of my leg cues; I knew I was in for the ride of my life on this charged-up, four legged, fire-breathing dragon! He was now prancing around with his tail up in the air, nostrils flaring red, and eyes the size of saucers!

All I could do was remain calm and sink my seat into the saddle as I tried to control this crazy lunatic under my seat, avoiding the other riders as we snorted, pranced and strutted out of control! Thankfully, the other riders saw what was transpiring and avoided us like a plague. In Arion's attempt to leave the arena we again came upon another of those show jumps. Arion couldn't handle it anymore and totally lost it! The next thing I knew, I was standing on the ground, holding his reins in my hand. What on earth had just happened? My mind was blank but I quickly looked around to see if anyone had witnessed the miraculous dumping of this rider by her horse; no one was around us! Apparently, they had been terrified by my pet dragon!

Arion was standing there beside me, all quiet and subdued, like a little lamb with a look of "What?" on his face! I patted him and looked him over to make sure he was not hurt; he was fine, not a hair out of place. Hmm. I then checked myself, again finding not a hair out of place or a speck of dirt on my gleaming white riding breeches! So, I mounted him again and headed over to the arena for my ride… I was *not* going to venture back into that warm-up arena! As we approached this arena, Arion started to get his blood up again. All he wanted to do was canter or probably gallop the hell out of there but I refused to let him have his way. Instead, I walked him in a circle while we waited for our turn. Finally the bell rang for us to enter the ring. All I could hope for was that he would stay in the marked-off test area and halt nice and square for the judges.

To say that ride was a flash in my mind is an understatement. Arion flew around that arena like a demon! He performed his Gaits, and in the Extended Trot his front legs were so high I thought he would bloody his own nose! I felt like I was sitting on a motorboat revving so high that the front end of it was up in the air! I must say that it felt great to ride that move! His Extended Walk was a bit rushed to say the least, but all in all he held it together *and* I stayed on, LOL!

The weekend passed by and on our last ride we were in the pelting rain and snow! When I had to salute to the judges, the rim of my derby hat was full of water, which splashed down all over my already-freezing legs. Arion was not impressed, but it was May long-weekend weather, what can I say?

Arion and I placed high enough in our tests that we gained scores to go towards the Provincials later that fall.

All in all it was an experience that I will never forget. I can honestly say: we came, we saw and we conquered.

As Bud would say, Arion was a force to be reckoned with, and I loved him for it.

#misshimeveryday #onehorseonelove #firebreathingdragon #forevermyhorse

Story 2

Not Funny!

Bud and I were a new relationship and had just moved into a new condo together.

I had one year of separation left before my divorce from Alfred would be final, and it looked like I was in for one helluva year! Alfred had broken into my apartment while I was away working, and things were not safe for me; I was ready to go into hiding if a new place did not work out...

Our condo was in the same neighborhood I had already been living in, and all the neighbors and store owners knew what was happening with Alfred. They rallied around me in an attempt to keep me safe, letting me know whenever he was driving around looking for me.

Bud and I had both been under a huge amount of pressure with our divorces and disgruntled families, so we hoped that this was a new start in lots of ways for us; where our relationship went from here was anyone's guess.

The new condo had two stories, with bedrooms and main bathroom on the second floor.

We had arrived home from looking after my horses in Bashaw, where they were hidden with friends because Alfred was trying to find and shoot them all to get back at me for leaving him.

We were sweaty and dirty from hauling hay and feed, and we needed to shower! When I was done with mine, Bud was next. As he showered, I came up with a brilliant idea to scare him when he came out of the bathroom! I squatted down beside the bathroom door, out of sight, listening for the shower to be turned off. The more I thought about it, the giddier I got, snickering to myself about how hilarious this was going to be...

Bud was a gentle soul. I had never heard him raise his voice, and he was always there being supportive in any way that he could. He seemed to take things in stride, but also internalized lots of his feelings, unwilling to give them a voice. We were, in lots of ways, polar opposites. (They say that opposites attract, and we could not be more opposite if we tried!)

Finally, the bathroom door opened. Out stepped Bud in his birthday suit. Within seconds, as he headed towards the bedroom, I leaped up, roaring, lunging at him and grabbing his leg!

Bud grabbed at his chest and fell against the wall with the look of pure horror on his face! His eyes were as big as saucers and he was as white as a sheet. I, meanwhile, was rolling on the floor in hysterics: even as I write this I am starting to laugh again!!

Bud, on the other hand, was not that impressed. He stayed leaning against the wall as his body slowly quit trembling, and color came back to his face.

All he could manage to say to me was, "THAT WAS NOT FUNNY!" Then he turned and wobbled to the bedroom with his hand on the wall to steady himself. He needed to calm his body down before he could even get dressed (meanwhile, I was still lying on the floor, laughing hysterically.) Finally, I was able to quit laughing uncontrollably, and went to the bedroom to get dressed.

Bud was sitting on the edge of the bed. He would not look at me, for I was still sniggering!

With all the stress that we had been under, and still were, each of our reactions were on extreme opposite ends of the scale.

To say that I was a livewire would be putting it mildly, and I think that through all of the trials and tribulations that we have been through, the one thing that Bud loves most about me is that I am never boring.

To this day, he is still not impressed about that day, and I still laugh.

Go figure that we managed to stay together!

As you read this story, Bud hopes that someone might find it not so funny. LOL

#throughthickandthin #survival #stillfunnyaftermanyyears

Story 3

Are these for real?

For my beautiful friend who left us too soon.

It was July 1, Bud and my wedding day, and my girlfriend Debbie was there to help get me ready for the big day.

Now, I am from the era of "Burn the bra, ban it, and stuff it away, rarely to be worn!" and frankly I liked it that way. But apparently Debbie had other ideas. She asked if I was going to wear a bra with my dress. I replied that I was not as it was a spaghetti-strap and I did not want bra straps showing. I think she already knew my answer and had come prepared to make sure that I was going to be dressed properly (in her mind). Thus, out came something she had hidden in her bag. She promptly handed me a box of sticky, gel-like pieces of rubber that were supposed to act as a bra-of-sorts with my spaghetti-strap dress. I did not know what to say as I looked at the box, then at Debbie, with all the expectation of success written all over her face. With a sigh, I said, "Thank you so much." and hugged her.

Bless her heart, but I had no idea what I was supposed to do with these wiggly pieces of rubber!

After inspecting the box, I looked at Debbie with questioning eyes and said, "Hmm, how do these things work?" Debbie burst out laughing, and there we both stood, laughing at both my naivety and her trying to explain how to use them! Finally, when the hysterics ended, Debbie offered to come in and assist in the application of the rubber thingies. I politely declined her offer of assistance as I did not quite feel comfortable having my bare boobs manhandled by anyone else.

For all you ladies out there, I had no idea that as you got older your breasts continued to grow. At one time in my teens I had fried eggs, and still considered that was what I had until I tried to apply these rubber "over-the-shoulder boulder-holders."

As I stood in my bedroom, naked, I read the directions on the box. With them in mind, I removed the first jiggly one and applied it accordingly, and next I applied the second jiggly one. I was not sure what effect they were supposed to have, but as I stood looking in the full-length closet mirror, my poor breasts looked like they had been in a fight and lost! One was high and one was low, they were squashed and mashed looking. They were not happy girls.

To say I was a bit lopsided was an understatement. Meanwhile, Debbie was tapping on the door, asking me, "How are you doing?"

I replied back, "Hmmm, fine." as I peeled off the rubber sticky gel-things.

So, again I looked at the directions on the box and tried one more time to apply the sticky rubber patches to my breasts. I had no idea if they were right-side-up or upside-down, both ways looked the same to me.

For all you riders out there, you get it. It is like looking at a bit for your horse; there is a subtle difference in the correct way it goes in your horse's mouth and the wrong way. If put in correctly, your horse responds positively, but put it in wrong and your horse refuses to listen and tears off bucking and snorting, with you in tow. I did not know the subtle difference with the jiggle gel-like rubber things – if there was indeed a correct way or a wrong way.

After applying them the second time, I stood and looked in the mirror again. As I looked at myself, I mused that at least they were the same height. I bent over and picked my dress up off the bed, slipped it over my head and adjusted it over my breasts.

Now, as I stood looking at myself in that mirror, I had only one big boob in the middle of my chest, struggling to escape the confines of the rubber sticky things attached to it! In frustration I pulled off my dress and threw it back on the bed.

Back to square one.

Debbie tapped on the door once again, asking if I was doing OK?

I replied that I was still working on it.

I have heard it said that *the third time is a charm*. I was not holding out much hope at this point.

This was the third attempt and time was running out and soon I would be walking down the aisle.

This time I turned the rubber sticky things the other way and applied them, hiking up each breast towards my ears. After I was finished, I refused to look in the mirror. Instead, I grabbed my dress and slipped it on, smoothing it out, and finally turned to see the finished result.

Staring back at me was this woman I did not recognize. Gone was the strong, independent woman who marched to her own drum, the woman who did not care what others thought of her and how she wore her own clothes! No longer was she comfortable in her own skin. Instead I looked at a woman who was caving into someone else's idea of how she should look. Disappointment in myself was etched all over my face. I shook my head and blinked my eyes to remove the vision that stared back at me.

As I scrutinized how I looked, I noticed that the rubber things were crawling out from under my dress and over the top! Not only could you see the rubber thingies attached to me, but you could also see my cleavage and the tops of my breasts.

I was very uncomfortable with people being able to see this much of my breasts. Without thinking of anything else but becoming ME again, I reached down into the top of my dress, ripped off each of the rubber thingies and threw them in the trash. I straightened my dress and my breasts settled back down to where they were supposed to be. Since I had very strong pec muscles from years of riding, my breasts did not sag or lay flat across my chest but stood proudly up front and center.

Debbie once again gently tapped on the door to see how I was doing.

I sighed, opened the door and replied, "Fine."

Debbie looked at me from head to toe and approved of the look. I did not have the heart to tell her that her gift was lying in the bottom of the trash can: some things are better left unsaid!

Within minutes, I walked down the aisle as I was meant to, and into a new life with Bud. We had lived together for nine years before he convinced me to get married again. Bud was the only person who actually knew and understood me, and he was just fine with the way I am.

Thankfully, so am I.

> #betruetoyou #makeyourownmould #falsiesarefake #overtheshoulderboulderholders

Story 4

Where did everyone go?

We were in Mexico with family.

With us were Bud's daughter Megan, Scott her husband, and their kids, Amelia and Charlotte. Also, we had his other daughter, Erin, and husband Scott (yes another Scott) and my daughter Tannis with her daughter Ahstyn (plus Tannis's boyfriend, we won't mention his name). Everyone was looking forward to the excursion we had booked: Snorkeling!

Now, I had never snorkeled in my life. I was not a very good swimmer and I hated water over my head and on my face. So would I actually be able to do this? I was not sure. Maybe I could just sit and watch the grandkids instead, since the youngest was only five years old. I would use that excuse if need be.

It was a long hot drive to Akumal Bay, where we were going for the snorkeling, and upon our arrival we were all sweaty and smelly. Everyone piled out of the van, glad to have some refreshing ocean air. That many people in a vehicle in the heat: well, you can imagine.

Our three grandkids were jumping around, all excited about going snorkeling!

Dread entered my body.

Since there were no change-rooms anywhere, everyone hid behind various vehicles, changing into bathing suits, towels up! That was quite the sight to see, I might add.

I came fully prepared and only had to whip off my clothes, as my bathing suit was already on. I was fine to go commando on the way back to our hotel after we were done.

Once we were at the beach, we were assigned a guide for our group. I looked around; the place was packed! People were everywhere, heads bobbing up and down in the water for at least a ½ mile into the ocean. *Hmmm, I wondered. How many sharks are in there?* I decided to ask that very question and was told that the coral reef stops the sharks from coming in. *Ok, I thought, I think I might believe that.*

Now it was time to put on the life vest and adjust our snorkel gear. I looked around to see where Charlotte, our youngest grandchild, was. Darn: no escaping the snorkeling now, for Charlotte was already in the water and roaring to go with her floating life preserver around her!

Everyone was wading out into deeper water while I stood there, thigh-deep, wondering if I could actually do this. Fear was gripping my heart and squeezing my airways when the guide turned to me and said, "Put on your mask and put your face in the water, then breath through your mouth only."

Easier said than done, Muchacho, I thought to myself!

I did as instructed, but the minute my face was under water I panicked and came flying out of the water like Jaws himself was spotted!

"Senorita, calm down. Just put your face in the water and breathe. It is easy," he said.

Memories of nearly drowning once while having swimming lessons was paralyzing me! I *had* to do this.

Once more, I tried to put my face in the water, and once more I felt panic overtake me. This went on for several more attempts. I was frustrated, the guide was frustrated, and I was ready to call it quits when I spied Charlotte out in the ocean, snorkeling away with Megan towing her.

Right then and there I decided that if my five year granddaughter can do it then so can I, fear be damned.

So down I went, staying there but hyperventilating and dogpaddling for all it was worth! Every once in a while, (actually every other stroke if truth be told,) I lifted my face out of the water to see where I was going and to try to locate the rest of the family.

Snorkeling, for me, was not an easy thing. Fear was gripping me tight in her embrace.

Thankfully, the water was calm because I surely was not. I think I finally felt more comfortable only when I spied a huge turtle and fish swimming beneath me. Wow, what a sight!

Now I was *mesmerized* by the sea life and I almost happily swam along, minding my own business until the next thing I knew, the family group was gone! I looked around for them, but could not find anyone! I thought *Oh well, I'll just keep snorkeling*: after all, they had to be here somewhere. As I was cruising along I felt a tap on my shoulder and nearly peed myself! I thought Jaws was in that water for sure! The guide had found me and was motioning for me to follow him back to my group. Being a slow swimmer, I could not keep up but eventually I found them all again. Once more, I was snorkeling, trying to keep an eye on them, still working on conquering my fears. However, there were so many other bodies in the water (banging against me or hitting me in the face with their flippers) that I lost them again as I navigated away from the other swimmers. After about an hour in the water, I realized that I was alone and far away from everyone else, including the family! This time, a lifeguard with his red floating preserver had found me. He motioned for me to grab the preserver while he swam back toward the shore, towing me in his wake. *Now this was more like it, and the view was pretty good too!* Back on shore, the rest of the family was apparently waiting for me, or so it seemed. Maybe they were just milling around.

Well, I was proud of myself for having taken that first step into snorkeling. Maybe I *will* try this again sometime: maybe next year when we are back in Mexico.

#snorkelingorbust #theadventuresofsomethingnew #niceview #jawsiscomingforme

Story 5

The Wild Things

2004-2019

Ty, our little dog, had both of us under his spell at six weeks of age.

He arrived knowing almost everything. He knew not to pee or poop in the house, not to chew on our shoes or drag-out dirty clothes around the house. He knew not to run on the road and walked right beside my leg when going into hardware stores and banks. When I stopped he would sit and wait for me to move, then he would follow.

As Ty got older he decided that he loved my lunge whip, which I used for working with the horses. Every time the end of the 20-foot lunge whip touched the ground, he would race to grab it! This was a bit harrowing, since I was afraid that he would get stamped into the ground by the pounding hooves! This thought never entered Ty's mind as he raced around beside the horses. There certainly was no way to keep him on the outside of the riding arena, where it was much safer. To Ty, if I was in the arena so was he. Ty had decided that this was where he needed to be. He became my shadow.

Fully grown, Ty stood only about 9 inches tall, and became very protective of me, chasing the horses if he thought they were going to hurt me. The horses were only running around and having fun, but if I was in the pen when they were horsing around, Ty felt that I was in danger and came to the rescue! He even decided that the moose that came around was fair game, and it soon became a matter of *me* rescuing *him*, although in his mind that was NOT the case.

He certainly was a big dog in a small dog's body.

We had purchased 80 acres of farm land to build our new home on. Our present place was just too small for me, both in the size of the house and amount of land we had. I needed room for my soul to expand, wide-open spaces and room to grow. (Sounds like the making of a country song!)

In the first few months on our new land, we had cleared the area for our house on the hill, and had the post and rail fences up for the horses. The water well was drilled, and we had built a pump house, work shed, and flower gardens around where the house would sit. We even had a purple marten house set up. We still had lots to do that summer.

One day, Bud and I (along with Ty and Tukker) headed over to the new place, only to find about thirty Llamas enjoying our flower gardens and lounging around! To say that everything was destroyed would be an understatement.

I was furious, and as soon as Bud stopped the vehicle, I jumped out and ran to the work shed to get my lunge whip to chase the Llamas home across the half-mile alfalfa field!

Little did I know that Ty had also jumped out of the vehicle when I did and was raring to go to protect his mom from these big, hairy, wild things that were threatening to attack his mom!

The minute I cracked the whip and started to chase them, Ty came running by and joined the chase! The Llamas, startled by this small, barking, black demon that was after them quickly decided that they could stomp on him instead of running. Now it became a race to protect him from the Llamas, who were not that concerned with me, but the demon in the tall grass was to be feared and killed!

Ty's blood was up and as there was no stopping him, I ran to keep him safe from the stomping hooves!

Suddenly, terror gripped my heart as I realized Tukker was not there!

Oh no! A cold sweat broke out across my forehead as the blood drained from my face.

I was quickly looking around for Tukker, thinking he too was in hot pursuit of the Llamas! Frantically, I spun around and there was Bud on the hill, sitting in the Jeep with Tukker, watching us!

I will not say what I was thinking at this moment in time as I was trying to rescue Ty *and* chase Llamas, while Bud and Tukker watched from afar! Hmmmm.

Since Ty was so small and the alfalfa grass was over two and half feet tall, he always had to stop, jump up to see over the alfalfa to where the Llamas were, then give chase again. He followed the trails that they were making, and at times a big Llama would stop and wait for him to appear so that they could attack him. When I saw this happening, I would run at that Llama, screaming and cracking the lunge whip!

Trying to keep Ty safe while chasing thirty Llamas through the field was exhausting! It felt like I was in a grueling marathon! My adrenalin was pumping as hard and fast as Ty's, but for very different reasons; mine to save him, and his to rid the place of those hairy fire-breathing monsters that were going to get his mom!

Finally, the Llamas were back down at the bottom of the field, along the field line, where they promptly jumped over and headed across the road into their yard.

Poor Ty was spent and suffering from exhaustion! He stood there with his tongue on the ground, barely able to move. I picked him up, hugging and cuddling him as I struggled back up the field towards our non-existent-house site. Instead of hiking the full half-mile, I cut across the field about ¼ mile to our driveway, which was also ½ mile long but much easier to walk. Bud and Tukker met us there and picked us up.

Both Ty and I were exhausted! As I collapsed on the front seat, Ty settled into my lap; both of us were panting from the ordeal as the adrenalin settled down. Tukker, in the meantime, was all excited that we were both back!

It is funny how our dogs take on our personalities: Ty was like me, and Tukker more like Bud.

#wideopenspaces #dixiechicks #firebreathingdragons #tytotherescue

Story 6

Are We Nuts?

The next project that Bud and I had to tackle was building a hayshed to store our hay. At the time, all of the square bales we had were stacked with tarps on them to keep the rain off. But the tarps were no match for the neighbors' cows that continually got out and ravaged our hay stack with their horns. So, we laid out our plan for the 22'w x 40'l x 14'h (for all you metric people that is: 6m x12m x4m) hay-shed on a piece of paper. Then, counted out the 18' 4x8 poles and lumber that we needed, and headed off to town to buy everything.

Bud hand-dug all the 4 feet deep holes, eight feet apart. Then we wrestled the 18-foot poles into the ground and cemented them with braces nailed to the poles, and pounded spikes into the ground to keep them straight. When the cement was dry we started to put up the boards along the side, spaced horizontally every two feet, so that we could screw the outside colored tin to the boards. Once we had that completed, then came the rafters to put on. So, with help from our neighbor (with his tractor), Dad, my nephew and three friends of ours, we wrestled all 22 of the 26' rafters into place.

Sometimes I felt like I was a monkey as I scurried along the rafters, nailing down 1"x4"x 8' boards to hold them upright and level. (Occupational Health and Safety would be *shuddering* if they knew, for there were no safety-lines on anyone!)

Once the rafters were all in place, then Bud and I worked on putting all the tin on the sides. When that was completed, we decided to move all the square bales into the hay shed, even though the tin on the roof was not started. I had to try to save what hay we had left before the neighbors' cows finished it off!

With the bales moved and stacked in my new hay shed, now came the time for Bud and I to tin the roof. The sheets were 36 inches wide and 18 feet long. We weren't sure how we were going to manage getting the sheets up the 14 foot wall, then onto the roof. With our long extension ladder in place, Bud put two clamps on the edge of the tin, then tied a rope to each clamp, joining them together about two feet above that. As he climbed the 18' ladder to the roof, he pulled the tin along with the rope.

Once he was on the edge of the wall (where the rafters were supported) he continued to pull up the tin, with me below the tin, pushing it. When the tin was straddling the roof, Bud pulled down on the rope. In theory, the tin would have flipped onto the roof and Bud would continue on to slide the tin along the rafters.

Instead, what happened was that the two clamps let go, and the tin came careening down the ladder, heading straight for my head! Bud screamed, "Look out!"

I managed to duck (otherwise I would not be telling this story, LOL) just in time as the tin grazed the top of my head, landing with a resounding **thud** into the ground and falling over!

Well, back to the drawing board.

On was my turn to come up with an idea. I decided to drill two holes in the corners on the one end of the sheet of tin, I left the tin screws half-way in. Next I wrapped baling twine around the screws, weaving over the top and bottom of the screw with the tin in the middle. Next I took the other ends of the long baling twine and attached both pieces to a rope. The rope was about 8' long, then I attached the other end of the rope to a light chain making it at least 14' longer so that it would reach Bud on the edge of the roof.

I had decided that keeping my head was more important at this point in time after our last attempt. Beside someone has to keep Bud in line, LOL.

With this new invention there would be no more standing under the huge sheet tin flapping in the breeze as Bud winched it up. As I stood several feet away I watched as Bud slowly and surely pulled the tin up the ladder. The moment of truth came as he once again tried to flip the tin onto the roof.

Would it work?

BANG! The tin landed on the rafters! Bud then scaled along, pulling the sheet of tin up so that I could climb onto the roof and help maneuver it into place. I think the hardest pieces to place are the end pieces, as you are precariously leaning over the rafters, trying to screw the tin down. Bud was not comfortable being on the high pitch of the roof rafters, 18 feet off the ground, so we switched places. He took over my role of getting the tin up to me, and I dragged the tin in place. Bud was able to screw down the lower ends while I scurried around, screwing down the rest. We still had no safety-ropes secured to us in case we fell, and we both knew that it was going to be a few days until we managed to finish pulling up all the pieces of tin.

Sitting on top of the roof after each section was done, surveying the landscape was rather cool. I could see the neighbors working in their yards or fields, and I could see everything in our yard as the sun's rays beat down on me. It was a fast way to get a tan as the sun bounced off the galvanized tin onto my body.

Ahhh, Life on the farm!

Over the years there was nothing that Bud and I would not tackle; we have built all of our own buildings, including that last addition of our barn!

So, how hard can it be? With a piece of paper and a pencil, you can create anything!

#newinventions #countrylife #donotloseyourheadoverajob

Story 7

If I had a Hammer

Our house had finally arrived on the new property and we needed a few stairs to get into it!

While the workers were finishing up on the inside of the house, Bud and I decided that we should make a front deck with stairs, since the construction guys were using the back one. We had put all the posts in the ground for the frame to sit on, and things were going along nicely.

Now, I am not sure if this is a common thing among couples who build together, but here goes: Bud and I seem to be able to share the same concept of what the finished project will look like (Ok, maybe that is a stretch) but for some reason, we cannot seem to articulate those concepts into usable phrases. It is similar to when I say' the sky is blue' and he said 'no it's purple.' This is one of those times.

With the 4 - 4x4 posts in the ground, two of the posts were right against the house under the front door. I was not sure how we were going to attach the 2x6 planking to the outside of the posts being that tight to the house. While I was thinking about this we attached the other three sides with nails and carriage bolts. Then we placed the support 2x4 along the four sides, stabilizing the deck frame with more nails; we certainly didn't want the deck to fall down. The time came to put in the back 2x6 planking against the outside of the post by the house. Now here is where the argument starts. Since we had placed all the other pieces of the framing up, there was no choice but to put this 2x6 plank on the outside of the deck frame. Bud wanted to put it on the inside, me on the outside to match the rest. Clearly, it *could* have gone on the inside, but I would always know that it was wrong, even though it would be hidden by the deck boards. Hmmm… I see a bit of a control freak here.

To my way of thinking, the board was already cut to the right length for the outside installation, and would require us to have to haul it back to the shed to recut it again. What we should have done, in hindsight, was install this planking first, but no, we did not do that! After all, this was our first deck-building project and it was" learn by trial and error."

So, with much grunting and groaning, we managed to bend the deck back a bit so I could hammer in the nails to hold the plank in place. With such a narrow space to work in, I was getting frustrated beyond belief! Bud was offering his own solutions while pulling on the frame, and I was hammering-in the nails. I only had a few more to go when the inevitable happened! My left pinky finger was not where it was supposed to be and down came the hammer! Does "Bang, Bang, Maxwell's Silver Hammer" sound familiar? Holy jumping Jehosefats!

The pain was *excruciating*, and I cussed and swore like a trooper! The tip of my left pinky finger was as flat as a friggin' pancake. The pain was shooting up my arm, and no amount of swearing was making any difference. Bud said, "We better get to the hospital and get that looked after." Through gritting teeth I replied, "NO, we are finishing this friggin' deck first. Besides what are they going to do about it, probably just put on a bandage then tape it to the other finger? I can do that here, so let's get this thing finished."

With a lot of determination and a throbbing hand, we finished the frame then started on the deck boards. When the deck boards were finished then we then set up the frames for the steps and screwed those down. By now, I was feeling a bit queasy. Plunking myself on the new deck, I surveyed the smacked pinky finger. It did not look that happy. I asked Bud if he would drive over to the other house, where we still lived, to get several Band-Aids so that I could tape two fingers together. I figured that if I was about to lose my lunch I did not need him watching me.

A few weeks went by, and my pinky finger was now a flaming red color, similar to Rudolf the Red Nose reindeer, including the blinking!

Bud was worried that I was getting blood poisoning. I said, "How would I get blood poisoning? The skin was not broken for anything to get in." He replied back, "Broken bones can still cause an infection." So, off to the hospital we went to get my pinky-finger X-Rayed. I was not impressed with having to probably sit there for hours on end, waiting to be seen, but I agreed to appease Bud.

After much waiting, they had finally X-Rayed my pinky finger. Now the doctor was sitting with me, showing me my smashed fingertip on the X-Ray, suggesting that a surgeon would be looking at it and possibly doing surgery. I asked him, "How can they do surgery when the bones are in so many tiny pieces?" I was pretty sure it was not possible as I looked at the X-ray and what my pinky-finger looked like on the inside.

So, with antibiotics in hand and a finger-guard on my finger, I left the hospital.

During the slow healing -process, it was fun to freak people out when I took off the guard and was able to actually roll the end of my finger around in a circle. Kinda gross, but fun just the same!

The things we amuse ourselves with, LOL!

Many bandages and six finger-guards were worn-out in the full year that it took for all the bones to fuse back together, and for the end of my finger to heal completely!

So, a word of advice:

Be aware, very aware, of flying hammers in tight spaces!

#smashedtobits #bemorecarefulnextime
#knowwhereyourfingersare #keepyourfingerintact

Story 8

A Willy of Sorts

To live out in the country is to live where the unexpected becomes the expected.

Since we had purchased the 80 acres, we had many, many unwanted animal visits from the neighborhood. With each animal's visit came destruction of sorts: cattle destroying the stacked hay for our horses, Llamas eating the garden, stallions and mares coming over and running through the lawns and creating huge holes in the grass, and the Jackass thinking he could to be of service to our mares! Pitbull/ Rottweiler-cross dogs, pregnant cats or Tomcats ready to fight! Then there were the pigeons and all the mess they make. Never dull, that is for sure!

After each visit we either had fences to repair, lawn to repair, or gardens to repair. The list was endless due to the many unwanted visits. After many years of these visits, we decided that putting up a gate at the bottom of our driveway was the only way we were ever going to have peace. Or so we thought.

For the past several summers we had had the neighbor's male donkey, Willy, coming every few days to see our mares. (not sure where or how he managed to get through the fence, but you could hear him before you could see him, running across the field, braying his head off, yelling, "I am coming girls! Here I am for you to see". Willy was a bit over-excited at the prospect of servicing our mares, and came with his 'willy' hanging down to the ground! He actually looked like a five-legged donkey; I truly believe that Willy was perpetually aroused. Now, our mares were not that impressed with Willy and his 'willy', and they would run the other way, terrified of this braying creature with five legs!

Once again, I would head off to chase the highly sexually-charged Willy back home to his own herd of mares! I guess he was extremely sexually frustrated, as he was too short to be able to do anything with the mares he lived with! How he thought he was going to have his way with my warmblood mares who were considerably bigger than those he lived with, was beyond me! But I guess "Nothing ventured, nothing gained!" was his motto.

This particular day, I had had enough of Willy and decided to chase him with the quad and the lunge whip! Off I went, in hot pursuit of

Willy as he was trying to crawl through the railing fence. Now, Willy was wily and knew he was in trouble, but the lure of the mares was pretty strong! He tried to deke me out by running only so far, then quickly turning to race back to the mares! Now, a quad can't turn that fast, but I was determined to send him back home. After several attempts, I finally had Willy running in the correct direction!

My daughter, Martina, and granddaughter Ahstyn, who was about six years old at the time, jumped into Martina's big ¾ ton 4x4 truck and barreled down the field in hot pursuit after us! We had a few hills and low valleys in our field, so navigating the turns was done with care as I chased the donkey, flicking the lunge whip as it bit into his behind. Willy now only had four legs instead of five, so running was easier for him! Keeping up a good pace, we all barreled down the field; Willy, me on the quad, my daughter Martina and Ahstyn in the truck, with Ahstyn yelling words of encouragement through the open window, "Go grandma, go!" as I flicked the whip on the donkey's butt. The next thing I knew, I was suddenly air-born! As I hit the ground, knocking the air out of my lungs, all I could think about was Martina, right behind in her big ¾ ton truck!

When I finally came to a stop, I just laid there, not knowing where Martina was, but hoping she was not about to run over me! Luckily, she had seen the accident and pulled up to see if I was ok! I lifted my hand to indicate that I was still alive, and away she and Ahstyn went to resume the donkey chase. Slowly, I peeled myself off the ground and staggered back over to where the quad had come to a stop. After checking to make sure the donkey was indeed still heading back home, I drove back to the house, thinking to myself that Bud was sure going to be pissed at me!

When I pulled into the yard, Bud was not around, so I walked around the house on the deck and sat down, overlooking the field from where

I had just come. Soon, Bud arrived and sat down. I asked him if he had seen the donkey-chase, and he replied that he had not, as he was occupied with something else. Whew! Relief flooded over me and I knew I had gotten away without him knowing what had happened! I figured there was no use telling him as he would only be upset and worried for me and would suggest maybe I should go to the hospital to get checked out. No, I thought to myself, 'let's just let sleeping dogs lie.' Shortly, Martina and Ahstyn drove back into the yard, after making sure Willy was back at his house and our gate was closed.

As Bud and I sat relaxing on the chairs, Martina and Ahstyn came around the corner. Ahstyn was bouncing with excitement from the big chase, and proceeded to tell Grandpa all about it, *especially* how cool it looked with Grandma flying through the air! To say that 'the cat was out of bag' is an understatement! LOL!

Bud whipped his head around so fast to look at me that I thought he had given himself whiplash! I assured him that I was fine and it wasn't anything. Ahstyn's version of the Flying Grandma, and my down-playing version were not the same story, and he finally conceded to discuss it later with me.

I must say that for about a week I sure was sore, but I would never say a word, for the phrase "I told you so!" was not something I wanted (or needed) to hear! I did learn my lesson: never chase the donkey with a lunge whip in one hand and the steering wheel in the other! One must have two hands on the wheel at all times and another person sitting on the back whipping the lunge whip.

I think that will be a memory to will last forever in Ahstyn's mind... *it was always exciting* to visit Grandpa and Grandma's house!

#flyinggrandma #accidentsdohappenwhennotexpectingit #maledonkeysareapain

Story 9

Au Naturelle

This story starts after I had decided to do some self-care by getting fake eyelashes put on.

My eyelashes are very short, and the thought of those luscious eyelashes you see other ladies wearing was too strong of an allure to ignore!

At 6 am the morning after getting the beautiful lashes glued on, Ty (our small dog) needed to pee *right now!* I was trying to open my eyes, but for some reason I couldn't get them to open: it quickly became apparent that my eyelids had *stuck together*! Gently, I tried to peel them open *at least* far enough apart to make a space between the eyelids so I could see to take Ty outside!

Now, when I say peel, I mean it in the literal sense. My eyelashes and eyelids were stuck together like a blowfishes' lips to glass (if a blowfish was near glass.)

Considering that maybe I should just wake up Bud and get him to take Ty, I felt for him on the bed. Hearing his gentle (LOL) snoring, I decided leave him be, and went back to prying open my lids as Ty was still snorting beside me, urging me to hurry up.

After this painful delay, I finally got Ty outside for his rendezvous with nature. Standing buck naked on the porch, I could only imagine what the horses were thinking as they looked at me, waiting for their breakfast.

I can hear it now: "Look, Mom's eyes are glowing! We'd better get out of here: she looks like a she-devil!" Watching them run down the field, I thought "Hmmm…No breakfast for you, knuckle-heads!"

Back inside I sat in the chair, now waiting for Ty to finish drinking water. Meanwhile, I decided to take my photo and post it on Facebook for all to see! As I was still waiting for the lapping sounds to stop, I had time to contemplate the day ahead.

Finally, with Ty in tow I headed off to the shower, hoping the cascading warm water would ease the irritating pain in my now glowing-red eyeballs! Some of you have actually seen that nasty picture.

The shower did not help, so next I decided to brush the lashes with the little fancy brush they gave me, thinking that would help. I have to confess that I might have combed a bit too hard, as a few fell to their death on the bathroom floor! Ok, more than a few, but it felt so good! I did not feel one bit sorry for them either. Lol

After getting dressed, Bud and I headed off to town in the freezing rain for my massage appointment. Now, most people would have cancelled this appointment, but no, not me. This was my self-care day number two. I needed to be limber for an upcoming airplane ride and frankly, my body was having a lot of arguments about how I should be moving at 61 years of age! I argued back, thus the harrowing 35 min drive to town.

Relaxing on the massage table, I knew what was coming. I embrace the massage-experience, knowing full well that the only way to relieve the knots is to get to them: more pain coming my way!

Some people have told me that getting a massage is like having an orgasm. Hmmm... that is certainly not my experience. What am I missing?

As the massage started I was resting my head on the backs of my hands, but soon I had to put my face in the head hole. OUCH! My eyelashes started to get stuck in the terrycloth wrap on the headrest! As I struggled to free myself from the grips of the headrest, the gentle hands of my massage therapist hit a knot! Now I am not sure which was more painful: ripping out eyelashes or the bloody knot in my back. Lol...Neither survived!

Now my massage therapist was slowly working my back muscles, her hands and wrist joints crackling like kernels of popcorn in a hot air popper! My bones and joints were not talking to her joints. I guess they are shy, stiff-lipped, "no speakie English", quiet as a lamb being led to slaughter for the supper table. Oh, the pain of it all! No orgasm was happening on this table! (I wonder what kind of massage they were getting?) Hmmm ... thoughts ran rampant through my brain as I tried not to hold my breath against the pain. Ouch! Another eyelash or two lost their fight with the terrycloth headrest! Meanwhile, my remaining eyelashes were still having their way with me, refusing to behave so I could enjoy the massage! (Well, as best as one can under pain!)

I think having a massage is like having a baby (for those of you who have gone down this path). You know there will be pain, but at the end of that hour or two or three you will have shoved a watermelon through the eye of a needle!! All worth it in the end, but not very fun during the shoving part.

Meanwhile, back to the miserable eyelashes! Finally I was able to put an arm under my forehead to relieve the eyeballs, or *eyelids*, more accurately. More eyelashes had succumbed to the terrycloth murderer. I could see the eyelash graveyard surrounding my head. Not a pretty sight.

Now I was thinking that I was going to look like one of those dudes that have gone bald, but won't admit it. Girls you know them, we see them everywhere. They have only one or two strands of hair on their head and they let it grow to about two feet long, then try to do a comb-over by wrapping it around the bald dome to cover it up. Doesn't work, does it? (Especially in the wind. Lol; he could strangle himself with those two whipping strands of hair that have evacuated his bald dome. Whoops, sorry... back to the eyelashes!)

Well here was my dilemma; I was thinking that by the time this massage ended, I was only going to have one or two lashes left! Did I prefer to still have those luscious beauties, or face the fact that I would be bald? Yes, I said BALD Eyeballs. Bald as a billiard. Hmm, what to do?

Finally the massage was done, my sinuses were relieved as well as my remaining lashes. I looked at the massage table headrest, and it looked like there was to fight to the death. Innocent eyelashes were laying everywhere! I can still hear their cries for help to be put back in their place. I wasn't budging. There was no sympathy here as I turned and walked out the door. Heartless I know, but one can only take so much. Lol

Next we were off to do the rest of the errands. My eyeballs were still cranky. Slowly, I began to pick at them, removing the culprits that were causing such discomfort! With one or two more gone, that felt better! But Hamm, there seemed to be another pesky one hanging in there, needing to be removed. Whoops: three more gone!

Looking in the vehicle mirror, I realized I had a bald spot on my eyelids! Now, ladies, that would not do, so, I evened them out. "Ok," I thought, "That looks better! I don't look like I was attacked by a weed-whacker and lost."

Meanwhile, Bud was shaking his head.

We completed more errands, but damn, here was *another* one causing problems! I eliminated that pesky eyelash, but whoops! I took too many again when we hit a bump on the road!

This was like eating potato chips: you can't eat just one, so the story goes! The same for removing rogue eyelashes, you can't pull just one!

Lol; I couldn't pull just one fake at a time with eyelashes protesting against the false friends attached to them, weighing the real ones down, being a bit of a drag.

You can well imagine the rest of the story!

So, how was your day?

#baldeyelidsarebeautiful #lessonlearned #neveragain

Story 10

To pee or not to pee, that is the question!

Have you ever wanted to go whale watching?

I certainly did! Whales, for some reason, held a fascination for me. Their size, beauty and grace in the water are astounding! I love to listen to their calls and hoped that someday I would get to see one up close in the wild.

So, we were back in Mexico, and there were several boat tours you could take to see whales in the bay. We decided that if we took a Zodiac boat tour, we were more likely to see whales a bit closer than in the large two-decker pontoon-style boats. We chose the 4-hour Zodiac boat tour.

The morning of our tour, we drove to "Vallarta Adventures" to catch our boat, and to be whisked away to see whales! As we left the marina and headed into the open bay, the wind picked up and the waves were rolling pretty well. Wow, I was in my element with the waves crashing, the boat pounding up and over the waves, and water spraying everywhere: what a thrill already!

This wild ride went on for about an hour before the tour guide received word that whales were indeed spotted about 500 meters from us. The driver spun the boat around and headed at breakneck speed towards the breaching whales in the distance. When we were about 100 meters away from them, the driver cut the engine and we watched as whales dove in front of us.

I was mesmerized, until I heard someone retching. I looked at Bud sitting beside me, and then looked past him to see a woman lying on the side of the boat, heaving for all she was worth! To say that she was green was an understatement, poor lady.

I thought that the tour was going to end so that they could take her back to land, but nope, the tour continued on. I felt so bad for her, having to endure another three hours of what she probably felt was a living hell, at least for her.

Meanwhile, the driver had another radio contact about another pod of whales! Off we sped again, whipping across the water, waves pounding once more! I loved it! I felt like one of those dogs that likes to stick her head out the window of a fast-moving vehicle, tongue hanging out, wind whipping through her fur, and drool flying everywhere! (Ok, minus the drool part, you get my meaning.)

Well, I had been very careful not to drink any liquid before leaving the hotel, as I did not want to have to go pee. But the pounding of the boat in rough waters had certainly created a bit of a problem for me in that regard. The more waves we hit, the more I had to pee! At one time, I even considered just peeing right where I sat since I was already soaking wet from the spraying water. Oh, what a relief that would be!

I decided no, I couldn't do that! First, it would smell like pee, second, it would be running all over the floorboards, third, Bud would certainly also get wet, and four, most important, I would know.

So, with legs crossed and teeth gritted, we continued to fly across the water in the hunt for whales.

At least I was not the only one in discomfort, as several more people fell victim to seasickness and were lying there, rolling and moaning on the floorboards of the Zodiac boat. Good thing I hadn't peed!

To say that those four hours were the longest of my life *would not in the least* be an exaggeration! I was never so glad to finally reach the dock!

Once there, I walked as fast as I could, with my knees tightly squeezed together, holding everything in. I am sure I looked like a wounded duck, trying to navigate the steep walkway up to the landing to a bathroom! The greatest feeling on earth is when you are finally able to pee after hours of bladder-pounding fury in the ocean so blue!

Next time, I will take one of those tour boats that have a bathroom on board, and watch the whales from afar with a tropical umbrella-drink in my hand. Just saying.

So, if any of you are thinking of taking a Zodiac boat tour, buy Depends.

You will need them!

#whippingacrossthebay #whalewatching #zippingalong #seasicknesssucks #thewondersofpeeing

Story 11

Free Falling!

This is one of those stories that I actually have to work hard at to find the humor in it.

I am sure it is in there somewhere; I just have to look harder to ind it! LOL; so travel with me on my journey with VERTIGO.

Now, I have to tell you *this* part of the story so you can enjoy the six-month healing process that I go through to get my life back after vertigo.

It was in the wee hours of the morning, the full bladder syndrome, UGH.

I slowly opened my eyes, lying there for a minute, then swung my legs off the bed. As I got up, everything went crazy! I sat back down, my head spinning, and couldn't focus my eyes.

"Maybe I should just lay back down for a while." I told myself.

A couple of hours later, the urge to pee was overwhelming, and once more I tried to get out of bed, only to nearly fall flat on my face on the floor! I hung onto the bed and called to Bud, "Bud, wake up! I need your help to go pee!"

"What? Oh, ok", he sleepily replied. As Bud came around the bed he asked, "Are you alright?" I replied, "No, I am really dizzy!"

With some effort, Bud managed to get me to the porcelain god. I sat there trying to stop the spinning in my head, but was not having any luck. Soon my stomach couldn't take all the turmoil, and up came supper. Now I was thinking that I had food poisoning from the lobster I ate while out celebrating with friends for the evening!

Bud helped me back to bed and suggested that maybe he should take me to the hospital. I said, "No, let me lie here a bit, and hopefully it will pass. Does food poison make you dizzy?" Bud replied, "No, not that I know of, anyway."

A few hours later it was morning, once again I had to go pee. I got out of bed, still dizzy. I stood, and this time I hit the floor! I lay there groaning as Bud rushed over to help me back up. This time, Bud said, "Let me help you get some clothes on. We are taking you to the hospital, NOW." I said, "OK, but I have to pee again."

Once more, we headed off to the bathroom to see the porcelain god, but by now I was really sick to my stomach! Neither Heaven nor Hell was going to stop everything from coming up as I sat there, weaving all over the place, hurling for all I was worth!

By now I thought I was dying a very slow death.

Martina was staying with us, so with both of them, one on each side of me, they managed to get me out of the house and into the vehicle. At that moment, walking was not something I could do. As I was seated in the car, moaning, feeling like death was around the corner, Martina handed me the garbage can just in case I needed it. Off Bud and I went.

OH GOD! The moving car! Again my stomach contents left my body with the force of a nuclear bomb! My head was spinning and my eyes were flipping upside down!

I thought I was dying.

We finally make it through the 30-minute drive to the Stony Plain Hospital, where Bud pulled into the ambulance bay. Immediately, an orderly came out with a wheelchair! As they peeled me out of the vehicle, the movement, once again, made me throw up, and I clutched my garbage can for all it was worth! By this time I thought my whole head was spinning off backwards. My eyes couldn't focus on anything except the blessed garbage can in my hands! The minute I tied to look somewhere else, all hell (and projectile vomiting) broke loose!

Placed in a cubicle with a narrow bed, I was now hanging on to the bed for dear life, fearing I would fall off if I let go.

The nurses quickly set up the heart monitor and everything else they could think of before the doctor came in to see me. When the emergency doctor looked into my eyes, he was having a hard time trying to focus on *one*, as they were both moving in opposite directions, flipping up and down. Meanwhile, I was white-knuckled, still hanging onto the bed. They gave me a Gravol to swallow in an attempt to stop me from throwing up, but that did not work. The pain in my ears was excruciating, my head felt like it was about to split wide open, my eyes nowhere to be seen in my head.

I thought, "I am dying!"

Now, with the help of several male nurses, the doctor decided to flip me over from side to side on the bed. For what purpose I did not know, but I did hear the doctor say something about my ears.

The four men grabbed ahold of me to sit me up, as I was barely in control of my own body. Then, suddenly, they threw me down on my side, back on the stretcher, and then they sat me up and threw me down the other way! Oh My God, I was nearly losing my mind as the world spin and weaved out of control as I hung on for dear life to the orderly. They continued to repeat the process, flipping me several more times, and when they were finished, so was I!

I lay on the bed, shaking out of control. The only relief I found was to keep my eyes closed! Only then would the pain in my head subside a bit. I guess it was because my eyes were not trying to hold focus on anything.

Oh God! I was wishing I were dead!

The doctor waited several hours to see if things would settle down, but I was getting worse by the minute! Now I could barely move my arms or move any part of my body without having to throw up. When the doctor realized that the flipping method was not working he decided that I needed a CT scan of my brain. This could only be performed at one of the major hospitals in Edmonton, but all the ambulances were gone. So, once again, into our vehicle I went with my garbage can in tow, and Bud drove to the appointed hospital. The moving vehicle was killing me. To survive the 40 minute trip, I had to keep my eyes closed so they were not trying to focus on the other moving vehicles and buildings.

I must say that I was not having much fun at this point.

If this is what death is like, I want no part of it, but I still thought I was dying.

After another several hours of sitting in the hospital waiting room, they finally wheeled me into the CT Scan. Once that was done, I was admitted into the hospital to await the results. About an hour later the new doctor came to see me and told me, "No brain tumor but you have a very severe case of vertigo; actually the worse he had ever seen. Go figure that I would have to be the worst case. I asked him what caused the vertigo and he said that sometimes it is unclear but usually it is because of the small crystals that are located within our eardrums.

Sometimes, these crystals fall off the ends of the hair located as a filter within the inner ear. They start rolling and banging into the other hanging crystals, causing them to fall also. These small crystals continue rolling around, affecting our equilibrium. Until they move out of the narrow canal, the vertigo will continue. So I asked, "How do they get cleaned out?" He replied, "They move out by themselves as they have to travel in the spiral of the ear drum. To do this you have to flip down on your side, dislodging the crystals to get them to move. Each time you flip from side to side, the crystals should start moving within the spiral, down to the wider part where the loose crystals no longer hit the hanging crystals.

In essence, shaking your head down sideways, or throwing yourself sideways down onto a bed should dislodge them. This is also achieved either by rolling over in bed, or sitting up and laying down *with force* onto your side on the bed, then repeating, going the other way." As I sat there, he told me to try to move them myself by flipping myself one way then the other. Visions flashed back in my mind as to how that felt and once more I broke out in a cold sweat as I tried to dislodge the crystals. When I had tried it several times I was once again throwing up so he then gave me a shot of Benadryl, and said that he would come back in an hour to see how I was doing.

Funny thing is, I have felt something moving in my ears for a while now and could not figure out what it was, like marbles rolling around. I guess those marbles were working their way towards the narrowest part of my inner ear and were now being very destructive! All I could think of was Super Mario munching his way along, banging on the inner ear hairs.

Bud stayed with me by my bed as I struggled to calm my body down and to get my eyes to stop spinning backwards then upside down. I must have looked like I was possessed with my wild, crazy eyes. All I wanted to do was go home.

When the doctor returned, he checked my eyes again. They must have started to slow the flipping because he said that if I could walk 50 feet down the hallway, I could go home. He said he'd be back in a few minutes to see how I made out. The minute the curtain was closed I was struggling to get out of the bed. With the IV pole in both hands, and Bud holding onto my waist, we walked together down the hallway. It was very slow, and I had to stop every few steps to gain control of myself, but we did it!

Teamwork at its finest, I must say. Benadryl was working to a point that I thought I might not die after all, or at least not feel like it! I was sitting up on the bed, fingers digging into the mattress to stop me from falling face first on to the floor when the doctor came back in and asked how I did. I answered, truthfully, that I did indeed walk down that hall and back.

Once we were home, Bud and Martina helped me back into the house and back to our bedroom where I collapsed.

I found that I was able to get to the bathroom on my own if I slid off the bed on my stomach, and then crawled on my hands and knees, leaning against anything solid. I was determined that vertigo was not going to keep me down and I worked hard to make it out the bedroom and into the other parts of our house on hands and knees. I had asked Bud to cancel my chiropractor appointment the day vertigo hit, as I was pretty sure I was not going to make it. A few days later my chiropractor called and asked me if she could assist me with the vertigo problem. I agreed, and soon I was on a program to help move the crystals that are rolling inside my cochlear, causing the vertigo.

It was weeks before I managed by myself to crawl into our living room to sit on a stationary chair. If I touched *anything* that moved, I was done for! Once, I touched the rocking chair and down I went onto the floor! Not a pretty sight.

I was making slow progress and I was determined to get back to doing my Pilates classes and riding. Vertigo was not going to keep me down. Unfortunately, it was months before I could actually walk upright with only the wall as my anchor. But the minute I was able to do that, I was determined to start riding again. With the help of Pilates to regain strength, and my chiropractor, who kept working on my back and my fused lower spine, I was heading in the right direction, or so I hoped.

Now, my back problems: that is a whole other story about Irish, and how that came to be. LOL

If life was telling me to slow down, it certainly made its point with vertigo, and I had no choice in the matter! LOL

#vertigosucks #cantkeepmedown #slowandsteady #determination #outofnowhere

Story 12

Which Way is Up?

I had been going to Pilates for a few weeks now and my life with vertigo was making things difficult, but I was determined to move forward. I had been making progress with moving the inner-ear crystals in both ears that had caused my severe case of vertigo. Today we were going back on the Centerline Cadillac apparatus, since I was able to hang on to it. We had tried the Center Line Reformer table, but that had been a bit of a disaster as I was in free form with nothing to stabilize myself when Vertigo struck.

So, with my trusted instructor, I approached the wicked looking table with all its straps and bars. Holy Moly; this should be interesting. I was hoping I wasn't about to kill myself!

After a few exercises to warm up my muscles on the table portion of the Cadillac, we then moved on to using the upper fleece-covered straps. Thinking this should be fun, I was going to do an upside-down push-up, hanging in midair!

Grasping the top parallel bars, I lifted up my feet and placed them onto the lower hanging bar. I then let go of one hand, placing it into the fleece hand straps and repeated this movement with the other hand. With my abdomen tightened, I was now hanging horizontally on the apparatus! Keeping this posture, I had to do pull-ups and then arch my back towards the top and lower my head, like the Yoga Cat pose, but upside down. The minute my head was lower than my body, **vertigo hit!**

OH GOD! OH GOD! OH GOD! My eyes were as big as saucers as a look of fear ran across my face! I had to get this fear under control before I went into full-blown panic! All I kept thinking was, "Don't let go, don't let go", as the room was spinning and swinging out of control! I worked hard to override my fear of being out of control, knowing full well that if I did not let go, I would be safe. I closed my eyes and struggled to control my breathing; breathe in slowly, release slowly. Breathe in slowly, release slowly. The thought of falling and hitting the floor was a sobering thought as I struggled to gain the upper hand over my mind. I was definitely in the 'fight-or-flight' mode at this point, white-knuckled and hanging there!

My instructor knew I was in serious trouble. She kept her hand on my back for reassurance, telling me I was going to be OK, as I hung there upside down with my eye squeezed shut. Finally, the vertigo subsided. Much to our relief, I was able to pull my feet off the hanging-bar, and then slowly slide down the sidebars onto the seating platform. As I sat there taking a few deep breaths, I looked at her and said, "Now that was interesting, shall we try it again?" Shaking her head, she said, "Let's wait for your next session to do it again."

My poor instructor agreed to help me overcome this demon, and together we worked at it. She studied her manuals about how to help her clients with vertigo, and I continued to try the things that she suggested.

Deep down, I *knew* I had to keep pushing myself! If this movement caused the vertigo to return, then that meant the crystals were moving again. This was good, because they had to be cleared out of my cochlear. Therefore, I continued to have three Pilates sessions weekly, in spite of the fact that vertigo continued to strike at each session! No pain, no gain, but I was *determined* to come out as the victor in this battle!

Eventually, after many more attacks and plenty of hard work and (stubborn!) determination, I finally conquered my vertigo in my Pilates class.

#veritgowilllosethisbattle #bestpilatesinstructorever #takingchances

Story 13

What do You Mean, I'm not straight?

Oh, to ride again!

The day finally arrived, and I was heading off to the barn to attempt to ride a lesson on a horse named Elijah, a 16'3 hh (hands high) ex-jumper I'd been riding before vertigo had struck. Elijah had no lack of "go", and at times liked to take control of the '"go" button! The speed that he liked best was cantering, bordering on galloping!

It had been four months now, and I could walk unassisted, be it not very straight, as I weaved like a drunken soldier.

I called Erika, my trainer, and arranged for a lesson. She was not as convinced as I was about me riding, but I was determined to at least try it, so she agreed.

Elijah was already in the barn when Bud and I arrived. This was good, since I didn't have to try to get out to the paddock to get him. Heading in to get Elijah out of his stall, I kept one hand on the wall (as a bit of an anchor to keep myself walking straight), then put my other hand on Elijah. We came out of the stall and down to the cross ties, where I would tack him up. Both Bud and Erika were watching me like hawks; neither one of them was excited about the prospect of my riding in my condition. Tacking up Elijah, I noticed both of them whispering to each other, chit-chatting about me, I supposed. With the horse all tacked up, off he and I went into the 20m x 60m riding arena where the mounting block was stationed in the corner. Elijah was a big powerhouse of a horse, and I had to stretch my left leg a bit to get on him. So, holding on to the front of the pommel on the dressage saddle with one hand, and the other hand on the reins, I lifted myself into the saddle.

OH SHIT! Vertigo hit!

I closed my eyes, put both hands down on Elijah's neck for security, and took several deep breaths to control my body. Erika asked, with concern edging in her voice, "Are you alright?" I replied, lying through my teeth, "Yes, just getting my bearings."

Next, as I sat there on his back, I pushed my legs down and made sure my feet were deep into the stirrups to stabilize myself. I knew that if I had something *solid* to lean into, I would be fine. The stirrups acted as that solid barrier between the ground and me. Once the vertigo was settled, I gently squeezed my legs and Elijah walked off, weaving and moving under me, following where my upper body was going. Smart horse! In my mind, we were clearly walking straight along the wall, but apparently to Bud and Erika, Elijah and I were doing a bit of slow, dancing, waltz-movements down the wall, clearly *not* straight! After a few slow laps around the arena, Elijah and I headed into a trot. Now this was really interesting, for as I posted, the whole building moved up and down like ocean waves, while parts of it were encased in big floating bubbles. It was really cool to see, but alarming at the same time. Once more, my brain was working in another direction. LOL.

Erika and Bud were watching with anxious expressions on their faces. You could clearly see that they were both in distress watching me. Once again I thought that Elijah and I were doing a great job of staying along the rails, but again we were not. Elijah, being the great horse that he is, was moving to stay under me as my upper body weaved from one side to the other! With my heels in the locked-down position in the stirrups, I knew that I was not going to fall off! In my mind I was on solid ground, not on a moving horse. After 20 minutes of riding I figured that I had done very well and was excited to talk to them about how well I did.

I was truly surprised when they both said that I was weaving all over the place, and that they were scared to death that I was going to fall off! Poor Erika was having an anxiety attack, and Bud looked like death had walked over his face. I decided that maybe I should finish my ride and get off; only to appease Bud and Erika, mind you. I had to think about the distress I was causing both them. They just needed to get used to the idea of me riding, because I was not about to let vertigo stop me!

That day, I was game to keep going a bit longer, for the feeling of being back in the saddle was great; I'd had another taste of freedom and had accomplished another milestone, in my mind.

Now the fun part the dismount. I don't dismount using a mounting block. Instead, I *jump* off my horse. This comes from the days of my youth when I rode bareback everywhere, and I did not want to have either of my feet in the stirrups during the get-down in case the horse bolted, dragging me to hell and back. As I sat there, settling myself after trotting, I needed to wait for the building to quit moving in waves! I watched, in my mind's eye, what I was going to do stop myself from falling when landing on the ground. Bud was standing beside the horse, ready to help me down by pulling me off over the side, but I shook my head. "No, but will you stand a few feet back from where I will land to catch me if I start to fall over?"

This was the moment of truth: I knew that if I fell now, riding was going to be out of the question for another month, and that was not something I was willing to accept! So, with a deep breath, I kicked my feet out of the stirrups, leaned over, and swung my right leg over the back of the horse. I then pushed off, landing with bent knees to absorb the ground contact, about a foot away from Elijah. In landing, I pushed my knees up into the straight position, as I quickly grabbed ahold of the saddle leg flap and hung on, trying to stop myself from falling while Bud put his arms around my waist to steady me. Voila! I did not fall!

Once I was composed, and with only a bit of spinning, Elijah and I headed off to the cross ties, where I would untack him, brush him down and put him back in his stall. As I was removing all the tack, I had to lean against the crosstie partition half-wall to keep myself steady. Vertigo was on the verge of happening again but I was refusing to allow it. Grooming down Elijah, I hung onto his mane as I moved slowly with the brush. Then, grabbing his tail as I walked behind him to the other side, I continued brushing him. Once that was done I dipped under his head, hanging on to the crosstie ropes to steady myself. Slow and steady was the game of the day.

I was actually very proud of myself that day: I came and I conquered.

Bud and Erika on the other hand probably gained a few gray hairs and wrinkles.

Elijah and I continued with our riding after that day, and each day I got a bit better, as my equine partner and I danced to my own drum!

#nothingholdsmedown #weaving #iamaweaver #veritgoorbust #elijahthewonderhorse

**Source: Story photo courtesy:
Cat Ballou- Photo of Lee Marvin in the 1965 movie.**

Story 14

Driving the Lines?

Six long months had passed, summer was here and the time to attempt to drive a vehicle was now upon me. Now this was a very scary prospect; driving in the fields and driving on the actual highway were very different indeed.

Our truck had to be taken into the garage for some repair work, which was going to take about a week to complete. Since I could not clone Bud, I was going to have to drive the truck 30 minutes to town while Bud followed in our Jeep. OH MAN! I was not sure if I was ready for this one, but I had no choice in the matter. What worried me the most was the safety of other drivers, as I didn't want to cause an accident! My perception of going straight was not functioning normally yet because my mind was still playing tricks with me on that concept. There was no choice in the matter, so off we drove, down our driveway and out to the gravel road.

As I was driving along, I was concentrating on trying to keep the truck near the white line on the shoulder of the road. Keeping it in my line of sight, off the front bumper, I felt would work well! I swallowed hard as we turned onto the highway, moving the truck over to the shoulder to keep the white line in view. Things were going along just fine. People were passing me, honking as I was travelling much slower than the posted speed limit, but I didn't care. All I knew was that I had to make it to town! With white knuckles on the steering wheel, I finally made it to the garage in one piece. I think I could have spit dust from being so nervous!

The following week I had to drive the truck again, taking it home. Once more, I was on the highway, but the white lines were not as clear on this side of the road, so I had to focus on the yellow line down the center of the road. Oh Boy! Bud was following behind me. I was driving a bit slowly at first, but eventually gained some confidence and soon was nearly travelling the speed limit. I knew that if I didn't get up to the speed limit, I might cause an accident because of the stupid, impatient people behind me. They were whipping in and out of the traffic in a big rush to get to where they were going. After all this was a holiday weekend, and people were heading off with their camper- trailers in tow.

It seemed like hours before we came to our turn- off. Now on a quieter country road, I breathed a huge sigh of relief to have made it that far! Once we arrived home, I asked Bud, "Well, how did I do?"

Now he looked a bit white around the gills and replied, "You were all over the road! I thought for sure you were going to get killed!"

"What do you mean? I stayed right beside the yellow line," I answered.

"No, you did not, you were weaving, but at least you did not cross the centre line into the other lane," he replied. OH GOD! What is up with my brain?

It would be a long time before I was going to drive again. My equilibrium was still playing tricks with me, my version of going straight was certainly not yet correct! I decided that I would certainly practice driving with our quad in the fields following the fence lines before I ever got behind the wheel of a vehicle again!

It took a long time to finally tame the beast called Vertigo, but I did it once and for all!!

#knowyouownlimits #crazywomandriver

Story 15

Some days, I wonder!

Mexico: Fun in the Sun!

This was the first Company trip to Mexico for Bud and I, we were staying at an all-inclusive resort and were wide eyed with everything that the Beach Palace Resort had to offer!

I am one who can't sit still for days at a time, so with company friends, we decided to go on an adventure of zip-lining through the Sierra Madre Mountains!

I was very excited about this daylong adventure and could not wait to get going the next day.

The adventure started off with taking the water taxi across the marina to "Vallarta Adventures", where we climbed aboard a zodiac boat and whipped across the bay at break-neck speeds to an inlet that housed a small village. I was certainly in my glory as the waves crashed and seawater sprayed us! I was extremely happy to be sitting at the front of the boat as we zoomed over the ocean waves, riding them up and down like a roller coaster. Thrilled beyond words, I embraced the speed and the feeling of flying!

Once we were dropped off at the dock, we were then led over to old army trucks with benches on each side in the box of the truck; they looked like banana-hauling trucks. (Maybe they should be called that for the adventure we were heading out on, as we were the oldest ones there. Were we *bananas, indeed,* to attempt this full day adventure? Hell, yeah!

Off we went, slowly weaving our way up the mountain trails to rendezvous with our guides. The road was not in the best of shape, with huge potholes and banks falling away as we climbed up the mountain. Thank goodness there were ceiling straps hanging down so you could hang on when we hit those potholes! Without them you would be thrown out of the back of the truck. It seemed like forever as we banged around in the box, bumping and crashing into each other. No longer were we all strangers after consistently ending up on others' laps! We had given up apologizing every time this happened.

Once we arrived at the drop-off checkpoint, we all could go to the washrooms and leave all of our personal belongings in lockers there. We were not allowed to take any cameras or bottles of water with us since our hands needed to be free during the adventure.

After everyone was ready, the guides walked us over to where our next ride up the mountain would continue, on mules! Since I knew how to ride I was given one of the more spunky mules. As it turned out, I was going to need him.

As we were climbing up higher in the mountain on narrow trails, one of the less experienced riders allowed his mule to overtake a few others, and soon we had mules running and riders screaming. As one woman's mule was taking off, I reached out and grabbed ahold of the reins to halt it while the guides got ahold of the others. All it took to start this dangerous situation was one person who wanted to be in front, against the pecking order of the mules! Each mule knows where they are to be in the lineup due to their own pecking order in the herd, and when this guy decided to change that, the higher ranked mules took offense. Hopefully a lesson learned for these wacky tourists.

The woman on the mule I had ahold of asked that I remain with her for the rest of the ride. She was white as a sheet and shaking, so I told her of course. Now my mule was not impressed that *he* was not in the correct order in the line, but with a bit of firm persuading he decided that he would allow me my point of view for the time being.

I instructed the woman on how to hold the reins and how to guide her mule. When she was calmer and understood, I let go of her reins. Together we continued to climb up the mountain trails. Soon she was more confident and told me that I was no longer needed. With this dismissal, I allowed my mule to traverse past the other mules until he was back in his order in the lineup. Finally, calmness prevailed and he was a much happier mule.

After a while, climbing and traversing the steep trails we came to a landing of sorts, where we dismounted from our mules. They were then tied head to tail in a mule line and off they went, walking in single, file back down the mountain. They knew exactly where to go and certainly did not need our attendance in it.

When everyone had re-adjusted their pants from where they had ridden up their legs, we then had to climb stairs. It did not take long for my asthma to kick-in. With the thinner air and the exertion of the steep climb, it was causing a problem. Gasping for air, I indicated for the other tourists to pass us, and Bud and I slowly made our way to the first zip line area. As I was gasping for air we watched the remaining tourists take flight across the ravine.

Now the fun begins. Bud and I were the oldest people on the tour, and maybe because of that the guides took extra care of us! We were strapped into the zip line harnesses and told to lean back and be sure to bring our legs up when we zipped close to the next tower. Closing in on the landing, we were to put one of our gloved hands back behind our head and grip the line to slow ourselves down. This would prevent a crash into the tree stand that was our landing target. Doing this too soon, we were warned, would make us stop before the tower, and then we would have to hand-over-hand in front to drag ourselves the remaining distance. Now this was something I certainly didn't want to do! Nope, I would rather go careening at top speed into the landing than stop on a dime on the spot marked 'X'.

Soon it was my turn, and as I was being strapped into the harness I was looking out over the gorge, thinking it was a long way down if my harness did indeed break!

Wow, what a rush! As I zipped across the deep gorge below, I couldn't help still thinking in the back of my mind, *I sure hope this harness doesn't break, plummeting me at top speed to the ground!*

Not a pleasant thought. As I whipped across the wide-open spaces, I felt like Tarzan's own Jane, flying through the air without a care! All I was missing were the screaming monkeys and roaring lions to complete the picture! In my mind's eye I was wearing the skimpy outfit that Jane wore as I cascaded along the gorge deep below me, doing acrobats in the air like a ballerina.

Ok, maybe I was not that graceful, but you get the picture.

Next was Bud's turn. I watched from the opposite tower as he was strapped in and pushed off the tower. The look on Bud's face was priceless as he also came zipping along. Fear of crashing must have been foremost in his mind as he brought his hand behind his head and stopped short about 20 feet from the tower! Now he had the fun task of pulling himself along the zip line to the platform. I must say it did not look easy. I believe right then and there Bud was ready to be done this crazy adventure I had dragged him on! Sadly for him, we still had a long way to go to be done. I, on the other hand, was raring to go!

We had completed about 4 zip lines when we came to a single line rope-bridge we had to cross, at which point we had to go up another steep incline to the next zip line. The rope bridge was interesting as there was one single piece of rope to step on as we hung on to the top rope, carefully stepping into the vertical ropes that held the two lines together. One slip and we would be in a bit of trouble, as it might prove difficult to try to get back up on the swinging bridge. Now the day was proving to be very hot, and sweat was running everywhere! Since my hands were so slippery, trying to grip the rope was a bit of a task, but I was not to be daunted! After all, I had to try and not show my age with those 20 somethings who were on our tour with us. What a fantastic day it had been so far. Meanwhile, Bud was less than enthusiastic as the day wore on. I guess being in your 60's did give him some credence for his lack of enthusiasm.

Next, as we landed on the next platform, we had to hike a ways to the next line. This time we had to rappel off the cascading waterfall and into a large pool of water! Panic immediately began to set in as I gazed over the cliff and down to the water. Not knowing the depth of the water was terrifying! I had visions of being weighted down and drowning as I had on full sweat pants and runners. As I watched how everyone else was doing it, I noticed that about six feet from the water, the line was let go and people fell splashing into the water.

OMG, I was about to die!

Now it was my turn. The guides put me into the rappelling harness and pointed to where I was to turn around and start the descent over the side and down the wet rock face. The hardest part was actually walking backwards over the cliff wall, trusting in the guide ropes and the harness!

Within minutes I was pretty comfortable, and was really enjoying it! I think I found a new passion of sorts! Slowly I descended as far as the six-foot marker, where the guides would let go of the rope causing me to fall. As I inched down the rock face, the guides kept ahold of my rope, allowing me to land in the water without falling. When I reached the water it was ice cold and it took my breath away! A sudden urge came over me as the water lapped around my thighs. (You know what I am talking about, and I bet if it were you, you would do the same thing. Ahhh ecstasy!)

Feeling rather flushed with relief, I slowly made my way over the slippery rocks beneath my feet and scrambled up to the edge of the water. Standing there, dripping wet, I watched as Bud slowly descended. Alas, he was not dropped into the water. I wondered if the water was going to have the same effect on him.

I guess that being the eldest, we were not treated like the young ones. Age does have its advantages!

Next, we were strapped into our zip line harness and sent over the other edge of the waterfall. Sitting right on the edge was a huge rock, which I was afraid I was going to hit with my butt! So, as I was heading for it, I lifted up my butt so I was horizontal to the ground as I went over the falls and down into a gorge!

A few zip lines later we were finally at the base of the mountain.

What a day!

9 zip lines later, two water fall rappelling's and a single line Rope Bridge! We all were exhausted. The final leg was a ½ mile hike back to the starting point with the mules. Bud and I were definitely eeling the effects o adrenaline withdrawal as we dragged ourselves back to the base camp along an old dry creek bed.

Once at the base camp we were able to change clothes, look at the pictures that the guides had taken, and purchase some if we wanted. When everyone had consumed their fill o water and ound the washrooms to empty their bladders, we were then back into the army trucks. At last we were heading down the mountain to the beach area where the dock was, where we had originally landed.

By the time we actually made it back to our hotel room Bud and I were done in! Thankfully we had a few days to store up some energy before we headed off on another adventure.

I must say that in all the zip lining we have done, whether Cancun, St. Lucia or Puerto Vallarta, this was by far the best one! As we have aged, Bud has stated that he could not do that again! I am game, but I'm not sure if I would survive it the next time as age creeps along!

#nevertooooldtohavefun #whatdoesagehavetodowithit

Story 16

The Irish Dance

2002-2015

I had owned my horse Irish for five years when I found out by accident from the previous, previous owner that he was a wobbler. It sure would have been nice to have been told this on the day of purchase, but sometimes certain horse people are not that honest.

To say that Irish was a handful is an understatement! He was proud cut, stood 17'1 HH (hands high) and was a thoroughbred with fire, and looked like an imported warm blood. I loved him for all those reasons and learned how to handle and ride him in spite of it all. Over the years of riding him, I had several vets try to figure out what his problems were; some days I could ride him and not have a problem, but the next day he would be bucking, trying to dislodge me! Or while riding, he would try to rub me off onto the wall. I had decided that in order for me to keep riding him I would have to put him into riding lessons, stabling him at the barn where the lessons were held. It was an hour and a half one way to get to where my trainer was, so commitment from everyone involved was key. Irish *hated* this barn but I could not figure out why. He had a huge stall and a turn out pen so what was the problem, what was going on?

One day I arrived at the barn to find Irish pacing his stall. He was very agitated, so I took him out and turned him loose in the riding arena. As he was burning off steam I went to the owner's house to enquire as to why Irish was in the barn. Normally, when I arrived my trainer was already there and Irish was in. But this time the trainer was not there, so Irish should have been outside.

She told me that she was afraid to take Irish outside because he would get too excited and run around the outdoor arena, bucking and kicking! So she had decided that he could stay in the barn until I came, which was every third day.

I looked at her and said, "So, Irish has been locked up in the barn all by himself for three days now?"

"Well, he is not my problem", she replied.

I could not believe it!

I retorted, "I pay for his stall and for him to be turned out every day, and you have not been turning him out at all?"

"No" was all she answered back. I was fuming about as much as Irish was as I stomped back to the barn. Just as I was opening the door, my trainer arrived. I asked him if he knew that Irish was not being turned out and he said no.

There was no riding Irish that day, and the following day we drove back and loaded Irish onto my trailer and left. Irish was going to another barn and arena down the road for a while until I could move him closer to home. I eventually found a local barn and arena and Irish was moved there. This was going to be easier as it was only 30 minutes from our house. I could ride him every day now and watch to make sure he was treated well. We had been at the barn for about two years now and everything was going along nicely except for the irritating bucking.

One day, after the owners had watered down the arena to keep the dust down, Irish and I were coming along the diagonal length of the arena when, all of a sudden, he tripped and went down along with me. We both landed with a thud! The wind was knocked out of me and my leg was trapped under Irish. What the heck happened? Bud came running over and helped me up as Irish was getting up. I checked him all over, I checked the ground, and nothing was amiss. Not wanting the memory of this fall to be his or my last memory of our ride, I once more climbed on board and headed off, walking around the arena. Both of us were a bit shaken, but by the time I finished walking him, Irish had settled down and my back had started to seize up.

The next day I went to ride again. Irish was doing fine, but when we were finished I could not move very well. I dismounted and with a painful throbbing in my back, I decided that I must have pulled my back muscles when he fell on me the previous day!

Then, the car accident happened!

I had whiplash, and now all riding had slowed down to a crawl. On what was going to be my last ride, I was finished and ready to dismount, but suddenly I could not lift my leg! My back had frozen! The muscles were locked in a boa constrictor-force squeeze, and the pain was taking my breath away! Bud had to come and physically pull me off Irish's back. For the next month this became our norm; I would be fine in the beginning of our ride, only to be extracted off by Bud at the end. Soon I was forced to quit my riding. Irish came home and I was miserable. I was in so much pain from my back and neck that for the next while there were many chiropractor adjustments, and Physiotherapy with those dam acupuncture needles. Oh, how I hated those things! They hurt so badly when the electrical pulses were turned on. As I lay there enduring the pain, all I could think about was getting back in the saddle.

Sadly, Irish never did get to go back to the barn, and I was off riding for a good year while everything healed. Then one day I got a phone call from the woman who had raised Irish. She asked me if I still had him. I said, "Yes, I still have him." She then said something that made a lot of sense, "Did you know that he is a wobbler?"

I relied that no, no one ever told me anything about him'" She continued to tell me that she had sold him to her girlfriend under the agreement that he was never to be sold to anyone. Also, he had fallen at the racetrack with a rider on him when he was in training at 18 months old. They figured it was because he was so big and gangly.

Somewhere along the line, something had happened to him and he developed wobblers.

There it was, the problem that I had been searching for, for years. Why he fell on me, why he bucked, why one day he was happy then the next angry. This poor horse had a constant headache due to the wobbler syndrome, and a back issue that had happened on the racetrack. If only I had known the truth about him I would not be where I am right now.

Since Irish was proud cut, he well could perform certain duties with the mares that are not appropriate behaviour for a gelding. Although a few of the more sexually-charged mares enjoyed bumping uglies with him, several others did not like this behaviour and all hell would break loose.

I remember when I discovered this trait of his. It was early springtime and I was sitting at my kitchen table, munching on toast, watching the pen of training horses. All of a sudden, there was Irish in all his glory, mounting a young mare! I think I choked on my toast and ran outside yelling at him to stop. Well, that was not happening, so in sock feet I headed off across the lawn, out to the pen, grabbing the lunge whip as I passed the watershed. I was yelling like a banshee and cracking the whip as I approached the duo! Irish was mid-thrust and not sure what to do as the whip came cracking across his ass with me screaming at him.

The rest of the mares that were trying to stop him were now running around, bucking and kicking. They seem to be saying, 'Ha, ha, you got caught.' Irish was strutting around, snorting and shaking his head at me while his sex partner was trying to get back to him. To put it lightly, the pen was in an uproar! I marched through all the manure and mud, over to the gate to the other pen, and swung it open. Then I headed off to separate the three training mares from him. Irish was not happy, but neither was I with him! I now had mud and manure all the way up my legs and my socks were caked! There would be no saving these socks!

Irish remained with us for several more years, enjoying life in the field. He hated being alone, and fretted whenever the mares in the next pasture disappeared out of sight. He was getting sore front legs from pacing up and down the fence line and continued to neigh day and night. He was losing weight and was just *miserable*; I am sure his constant headaches were not helping.

So, one day I decided that either I would get another gelding for him or find him a new home. I searched and searched, but could not find anyone who wanted to get rid of a gelding to be used as a companion. As a result, I was forced to look at just giving him away to someone who wanted a companion gelding. I had lots of enquiries, but everyone thought that I was some stupid women who did not know anything about horses, and that they could ride Irish. I tried to explain why they could not, but when they looked at him they could not see the problem. He was big and strong and gorgeous. They thought they hit pay dirt, but I refused all their offers.

Finally, a young couple responded to my ad that wanted Irish. They sent me photos of other horses in their pasture and showed me where Irish would be living. These two were all about saving horses, and loved to have them around to look at. I told them all about Irish, including the fact that he had wobblers and that he was NOT to be ridden. He was only to be a pasture mate in the herd. They understood fully, so thinking I was doing the right thing or Irish, I gave him to the young couple, and sent Irish off to his new home, with tears rolling down my face. I wanted a better life for him, not that one that he had at the present time. The couple even sent me photos of him with the herd! But unfortunately, this was all a ruse. Irish, and I am sure all the other horses they had been given, was sold to the slaughterhouse. Now I understood why I could not find a companion horse for him.

This was proof that not all horse people are honest!

When I realized what had happened, I sent off a letter telling them exactly what I thought of them and their underhanded tactics! Sadly, that did not save Irish, who deserved to have a better life than what we humans had given him. This is one regret that I will take to my grave. I hope that one day Irish and I will meet again under better circumstances.

#fortheloveofahorse #abetterlife

Story 17

Are you Insane?

Once more, we are at it; this time it was building my barn.

I have always wanted my own riding arena and barn where I could work my horses from home. When I think of how much money was spent over the years, I shudder! All the money could have been used for my own place instead of paying for someone else's dream. Now, to be sure, all the designs of barns I had created were a significant amount of money, the kind of money one does not have lying around, or at least I didn't.

One day, Bud said that maybe, *someday*, we could build my dream barn. Screeech! Halt! WHAT! The wheels in my head were now set in motion and the barn building had already begun. The words "maybe" and 'someday' did not register in my brain: that someday was here NOW! All I had to figure out was *HOW*?

The barn was going to be a pay-as-you- go project, and Bud and I were going to have to build it ourselves in order to save money.

So, how hard can that be? I would soon realize that Bud and I had aged a bit, (even though I fight that cursed age-thing!, and with just recovering from vertigo over the past year and a half: Dam Hard!

We had already built several sheds; a tack shed and the hay shed, so this should be a snap. So, with my trusty pencil and graph paper, the barn was laid out with all the doors and windows in place. Then all the lumber, including how many rafters we'd need to buy, was figured out and marked down. This was our blueprint.

In that first summer we had to relocate parts of the post and rail fence line to make room for the new barn. Next we had loads of clay dirt hauled in to level the sloping ground where the barn would sit. This had to settle over the winter and pack down. Spring time came, and if you stepped onto the clay you sank up to your knees, so we had to wait until late spring before we could stake-out and square-up the string lines for the walls. Next we (actually Bud) had to hand dig all the holes for the 4x8x12' posts that would be the start of the walls. This was going to be a pole barn. In settling the outside frame for the walls, we had to make sure that everything was straight and square. Not so easy with stretchy string and wind! After all the 18 big posts were in the ground and the cement was cured, next came the 2x6x16' strapping for the walls, and then hopefully: putting up the rafters.

Bud had said that the minute I started this barn project there was going to be no peace because I would be pushing to get it finished! I assured him that we would take our time. LOL: famous last words out of my mouth!

Now *this* was the year of Bud's family reunion at our place, and I was keen to have at least all the framing done, plus the rafters on and maybe tinned. Bud was of a different mind, I might add.

That whole summer we slaved away at getting the frame up and to make sure that the building was square. The August long-weekend was getting really close, and all that was left was to put the 34' rafters up on the roof. Neither Bud nor I had a clue as to how we were going to do this by hand. We thought about renting a crane of sorts after the reunion was done, but then again, neither of us knew how to drive one! All we had was our big tractor, and the bucket would not lift the rafters high enough to reach the roof. Our salvation came when our next-door neighbor, Dean, came over to see what we were doing, and he offered to help us put up rafters! Dean said that he had a 10' extension that we could use; we just had to slide it over the top of our front-end loader round bale spear. So, as Bud climbed up the strapping on the west wall, and Dean climbed up on the east wall, I hooked-up the sling onto the end of the extension and lifted the first rafter at the highest point.

My job was to maneuver through the 8' wide doorframe (since we had taken off all the headers and the two top boards for the end rafters to sit on), and then place it up on the walls for the boys to screw into place. We managed on the first day to get half of the rafters up The space to get in with the tractor was getting smaller once we had the end wall up. As I was trying to maneuver the last rafter on the first day, I could not see that it was caught on the wall strapping. All I heard was SNAP! You know that sick feeling in your stomach when you know you really screwed up big time, and then the feeling turns into anger? Well that was me: I was furious with myself! Now what were we going to do? Ordering a new rafter was not that easy, and to get it hauled out was going to cost over $300.00. I backed out of the doorframe with my broken rafter flying in the air. We all were done for the day.

That evening I went outside to fix the broken rafter. We had a few spare plates left over from building rafters for the smaller buildings, so I figured, why not try it? I cut off the broken piece and fitted a new board in place, then placed a bracket over each end and started pounding the rivets on the bracket in place. Once this was done I took another piece of 2x4, about 4 feet long, and screwed that over the mend, then flipped it over and added another bracket on the opposite side with another 2x4 x4', repeating the mend. Voila, good as new! I was pretty proud of myself for fixing my error. The next day Dean came over and we finished the job. Now all we needed was the tin on the roof, but that was going to have to wait as the reunion was in a few days and Bud's sisters were arriving the next day to have time to visit.

We had invited to the reunion my Dad and Olive, and new friends Marta and Don who were originally from Arkansas and had been living in Edmonton for the last 10 years. We were all sitting around, chatting about the new barn, and I said the next job was to tackle the roof. To our surprise Marta said, "Oh. Don and I will come out and help y'all." I was blown away by such a sincere offer to help us, but I also was not sure how they were going to help! Marta was a very fashionable lady with the long nails and makeup, a polar opposite of me, who, well let's just say I am not that fancy. It was not long after the reunion was over that Marta called and asked what day we were going to put the tin on the roof. So, with the date set in accordance with the weather (wind and tin do not mix well) Marta and Don arrived in work clothes ready to do whatever was needed.

Don and I were stationed on the roof, Don near the bottom end of the rafters, closest to the wall, and me up high in the rafters. With our work belts full of tin screws and power drills in hand we were ready for when Marta and Bud hauled over the 16' sheet of tin. We were about half way across the east side of the roof when it happened!

I was straddling two rafters; the tips of my shoes were barely on the end of the bottom part while my body was perched vicariously over the top, (not in a good position) when vertigo hit!

It was a 14' fall to the ground, so I struggled to stay as calm as I could while wave after wave of rolling motion hit me! I was hanging on for dear life when the spirit of my deceased brother, Bruce, appeared! He stayed with me and told me that I was going to be ok, and to just hang on and not let go of the rafters. I was white knuckled; holding on, for my life did depend on it! I was focusing on just slow breathing for what felt like an hour (probably only minutes) as everyone stopped what they were doing and watched in horror as I struggled with vertigo! There was nothing anyone could do, and no one could get to me without considerable effort and possibly hurting themselves in the process. As the vertigo was passing, I was able to focus again, and from my rafters in the sky I could see Bud standing below me with fear etched all over his face! He was ready to call it a day, but I insisted I was Ok and that we should finish the east side, as tomorrow the west side was going to be done. Make hay while the sun shines.

With the help of friends, we managed to get everything done that year that needed doing. Next year we start the plywood on the outside, windows and doors, then work on the inside. Never nothing to do living on our farm of dreams.

I think being married to me is probably one of the toughest and easiest things Bud had ever done. I am certainly not dull and nobody can accuse me of being sane. LOL

#makinghaywhilehtesunshine #neveradullmoment #brucetotherescue

#greatfriends #surprises #spiritscalling

Story 18

How was your night?

Bud's night was as thus:

We have two little house dogs, Ty and Tukker who sleep on our bed with us. It is 3:00 am and Ty needs to pee real bad. He is standing up by Bud's head, trying to wake him up with his whiny and huffing and blowing stuff through his nose landing on Bud's face.

Bud wakes up and gets up begrudgingly; as I try not to as I am not that fond of the dark (old issues from a long time ago.) He scoops up Ty who is deaf and blind, and heads for the bedroom door.

Tukker keen on protecting the property from marauding critters that should not be there outside in his yard, decides to follow.

Bud stumbles down the hallway in his drowsy state, heading for the back door of the house. He unlocks the door and walks across the patio to the steps, where he will go down to let Ty go pee in the grass.

At the bottom of the stairs that lead to the grass is the skunk who has been stinking up the yard and stealing the cat food that is set on the deck (under a plastic dog shelter in the shape of an igloo) by the back door.

Tukker, who is a keener, sees the skunk before Bud does! Bud happens to still holding a squirming Ty, who still has to pee really badly, as he is about to take the first step down he is awakened from his sleepy stupor by Tukker's furious barking! Bud sees the skunk just before Tukker, the ferocious watchdog (note he is about 12" tall), takes off down the steps in a hot pursuit and after the skunk!

Tukker is envisioning the chase: the skunk is running for all it is worth while Tukker is nipping at its butt, encouraging it to run faster. Oh the chase, such a glorious thing it is! After all the skunk should not be there and Tukker is being a good watchdog.

As Tukker descends the steps in his excitement of the great chase to this invader, Bud gives a blood curdling scream for Tukker to "STOP!"

What is amazing is that Tukker actually listens mid-stride down the five steps to the ground, and is now standing growling and barking. The skunk slowly turns proudly showing his hinny and his scent glands that are load and ready to be dispersed if required. Then the skunk decides that there is way too much noise and saunters off to a quieter neighbor.

Bud is much relieved as he watches the skunk depart, thinking that if things had gone wrong he will be sleeping outside, buck naked with his free 'willy' dangling in the breeze with only two stinking dogs keeping him warm.

Misery loves company.

Crisis adverted, he takes Ty down the steps to go pee while Tukker is too busy sniffing around where that ferocious-looking intruder had dared to walk on his lawn. When both dogs have finished their business they all come back to bed, thankfully smelling no worse for the experience.

Lol, gotta love country life, where you can stand buck naked in the middle of the night on your porch for only a skunk to see your naughty bits flapping.

#peppylaphew #guarddog #bucknaked #freewilly #catfoodstealingskunk

Story 19

The Jesus Pillow

H ere I was, sitting in the lobby of the Granville Island Hotel, Granville Island, Vancouver, British Columbia, waiting for Jo to arrive, since we were sharing a room.

As one of the speakers for her Frock-Off event, I was looking forward to having a few days away in the sun instead of the snowy February here in Alberta. Now the B.C. weather was not all that great, but then again it was an improvement on snow, or so I thought as I watched big rain clouds moving overhead.

Since I really didn't know when Jo was arriving, I decided to leave the lobby and wait for her in our room. With my room key in hand, I entered the elevator and pressed the third floor button... nothing happened. Hmmm. I pushed the button again, and again nothing happened, so I exited the elevator and walked over to the main desk and reported that the elevator was not working. The receptionist informed me that I had to start the elevator with my key. Really? How strange, I thought, as I walked back to the elevator.

I flashed my key, pressed the button, and *Viola*, up we went! Ok, I don't get out much and this was the first time I met this kind of elevator!

Undaunted, I arrived on my floor and proceeded to search for our room, which was supposed to have two queen beds and a view of the harbor. After all, why come all this way to look at a parking lot when the ocean was right there? After many, many turns and narrow walkways, I finally found our room, only to be greeted with one King-sized bed and the breathtaking view of the parking lot! We were staying in what they called "The Attic Loft" room; not as fancy as it sounded, and certainly *not* what I had reserved! So, back down I went to the lobby to inquire why I had *this* room instead of the one on my registration! Where was my ocean view?

Sadly, I was told, "Oh, if you want that kind of room the cost is $200.00 more."

"What, are you kidding me? This is not what your advertisement said," I replied. My room was already $300.00 per night!

"Oh, we changed everything, as we had requests for those rooms by guests who stay here frequently." was her clipped reply.

What crap, I thought to myself as I entered the elevator again, only to discover I had left my key on the desk in the room. Grrrr!

Once more, I returned to the desk to ask for assistance, only to see Dr. David Suzuki standing there, waiting to be served! (Maybe Dr. Suzuki was getting the kind of room I had reserved. If so, I hope he had a crappy sleep!)

So far, I was not impressed.

I followed the receptionist back to the elevator, where she flashed her card and quickly exited as the doors were closing and up I went to our attic room to wait for Jo to arrive. Interestingly enough, I was now standing in front of my room with no key! So, down I went *again* to the lobby to get another key. Man, was this *ever* going to stop?

After much waiting, the receptionist again asked if she could help me. I told her that my room key was still in my room and I needed a spare. As I was waiting, Jo walked into the hotel and up to the reception desk. In short order, Jo had her key in hand and once more I headed up to the third floor! This time, with Jo following me to our attic room, I opened the door and entered with her behind me. One look at me and we both burst out laughing at what our room looked like compared to what it was *supposed* to look like. With the lovely view of the parking lot, the threadbare rug and the breeze from outside whistling through the cracks alongside the windows, I figured we were going to be in for a treat in this attic room. The only thing missing was a spirit of some long-ago dead person paying us a visit!

Later that evening we had supper in the main dining room that overlooked the harbor. As I gazed out the window at all the different boats that people were living on, big white snowflakes started to fall. The breeze turned into a fierce wind picking up the light snow, and soon a *blizzard* was in full force outside! So much for getting away from the snow! After watching the snow pile up, we headed back up to our "Attic Loft. Before dinner, we had spent considerable time and energy setting up the conference room for tomorrow's event, so both of us were looking forward to relaxing a bit. Jo was not feeling particularly well and I was exhausted from the early flight, so we decided to turn in early. Now, Jo and I had never shared a room together let alone a bed, but as we were both women I figured all would be well.

Even though our bed was a king-sized, on it were those huge giant pillows, the size that Gulliver (in Gulliver's Travels) would use. There was no room on the bed for anything else, including people, with these huge pillows on it! I suppose they were there for decoration of sorts.

Jo had finished getting herself ready for bed, and now it was my turn in the bathroom to get ready. When I came back into the bedroom, Jo was laying on her back on one side of the bed with her laptop open. Next to her was this giant pillow, which now left a very small sliver of space for me. Now, I am not as tiny as Jo, so this was going to be interesting! I was not sure how I was going to fit in that little space: maybe if I laid on my side with my leg dangling over the edge to touch the floor, I might not fall off!

I settled on the bed, trying to squeeze as close to this humungous pillow as I could, but was not having any luck. Finally I turned over, sat up and said, "What's with this pillow?"

She looked at me and replied, "I don't want to appear to grope you in the night, thinking you are Michael" (her husband).

I burst out laughing, and suddenly we both were laughing hysterically!

Through tears I replied, "Do you think this Jesus-size pillow is going to save me?"

Again, we were in hysterics, laughing out of control.

Jo answered, "I didn't want to startle you in the night if I rolled over and my arm flung over at you."

I replied, "No worries on that front!" I replied. "With your Jesus pillow in the way, one would have to climb over a mountain reach me over here!" Again, laughter filled the room. Either we were both extremely tired or both insane!

Meanwhile, Jo was starting to slur her words a bit. She said that she had taken pills the doctor had given her and was feeling really groggy. Within seconds, Jo was out like a light.

With her out, I grabbed the Jesus pillow and flung it onto the chair! I then settled down comfortably on the bed and drifted to sleep.

The next morning, I awoke to find Jo in the same position that she fell asleep in. I don't think she needed to worry about groping anyone, as she was in a comatose state! After a fashion, Jo started to stir, still groggy from the meds she had taken.

The following night, the Jesus pillow stayed on the chair and a much smaller version was set in place in between us. At least this one did not take up nearly the whole bed.

To this day, whenever we travel and stay together, we laugh about the Jesus pillow and how it was there to save me from her.

#gulliverspillow #outofcontrollaughter #neveradullmoment. #firsttimeroomies

Story 20

Wonder Womannnn?

I won't say that I make a good patient, and I won't say that denial is not my middle name. So goes the story of how I broke my ankle.

There were two of us, Erika and myself, taking the Energy course on a cool winter weekend. We were in the second day of the course about being an empath, connecting to our guides and the energy around us. We had just finished lunch and I was heading towards the staircase to go back down stairs to have our dessert:

Decadent cherry cheesecakes, mmmmm good! The stairs were the narrow kind that you find in older homes, the ones that you almost have to step sideways with your foot in order to go down the steps. The rug was also the older kind, a shag type. Remember the days of the mullet haircut, short in the front and long at the back? This carpet resembled that look: worn-out down the middle with the sides retaining their youthful length. The rail on the right side had been replaced with a track railing for the chair lift, which was folded-up at the bottom of the stairs. For some reason, I had stopped at the top of the stairs, holding two dessert plates, when I heard this voice in my head say, "Head first or feet first?"

Within a blink of an eye, the next thing I knew I was flying down the stairs on my butt, or rather with my right leg under me, acting like a ski, and the left leg sticking out like a backwards rudder on a boat! In my hands were the two cheesecakes.... when I crashed at the bottom of the stairs the cheesecakes went flying! My ankle cracked, but appeared to still be in a normal-looking position. Everyone came running to see if I was OK. *Enter the "Super Woman" cape!*

I sat there for a few moments, marvelling at how good my bones were, for nothing was broken. I thought to myself, "Well, at least I don't have to have a bone density test now." The things we think about in times of extreme pain are crazy and the denial is even worse. Thyra, the course instructor, helped me get up, and with her assistance I hopped towards the bathroom to attempt to clean up all the cheesecake that was covering me! In hindsight, I should have told them to get their spoons out and eat it off me, but alas, I did not. As I was sitting on the bathroom throne, wiping off my clothes, contemplating my ankle and the sprain I thought I had, I decided to continue with the course for the afternoon. Maybe directing some healing energy to my ankle all after-noon would ease the pain and swelling.

After all, I was here to learn about that, so what better time to repair myself? Finally, four hours later, the course was over. It was time to go home, but I still had to get up those stairs in order to do that! Thyra's dad suggested that maybe I should use the chair lift since it was down there already, but I refused. I felt that I would be imposing on them. Besides, I also thought, how can I use that? I am not that old and it is only a sprain. So, with the help of Erika, my fellow course combatant, I stubbornly managed to get up those stairs. I think that was the longest staircase in the world. To say that I felt sick to my stomach was an understatement, but stubbornness prevailed. *WONDER WOMAN and her Cape of Denial!*

Now let me explain the *Wonder Woman* thing. Bud, my husband, calls me Wonder Woman all the time when I am doing something really smart or, frankly, really stupid. (In his opinion, never mine.) So here I was, 'Wonder Woman'ing' it again. Denial was my friend right now. As I hobbled to the car and Bud, I could see him shaking his head in disbelief. As I was getting in, he laughed and said, "Yesterday you helped Erika out, and today Erika had to help you out. What kind of course was this again?" Begrudgingly I told Bud what had happened, and that I sprained my ankle. Bud, being Bud, asked if I wanted to go to the hospital for x-rays to see if it was broken. I flatly refused to go to the hospital, to just sit there for hours on end, waiting to be told that I sprained my ankle! No thank you. So, off toward home we headed, me refusing to show Bud that I was in any pain as he purposely (probably not, but still...) hit every bump and pothole in the road!

The next day I sent Bud into town to buy me a set of crutches so I could move around the house. The umbrella I had been using was not faring very well as it had bent due to being used as a crutch instead of the job it was intended for. When he arrived home, I tried out the crutches, which, by the way, were way too long for me even when adjusted to the lowest notch. These crutches must have been built for the Friendly Giant! So, as I was trying to maneuver King Kong sized crutches, they got caught on the rug and down I went over top of the arm of my chair! The pain was unbelievable! There I was, stranded upside down while Bud sat on his chair looking at me. I swear he had this smug look on his face, the look that said, "I told you so." After a very restless night, I conceded, and in the morning off to the hospital we went to get my ankle x-rayed.

Several hours later, the emergency doctor came in. He asked what color of cast I would like, and informed me that I would more than likely need surgery. Again, denial was my friend and I told him that he was crazy; I only sprained it. With this look of utter disbelief, he whipped out the x-ray and revealed my broken ankle. Not only was it broken but it was separated also. (Did I mention that I am not a good patient? I hate being sick or broken - it drives me crazy!) He informed me that the surgeon would be calling me to discuss the surgery in a few days. I was not impressed and still believed that they were clearly wrong: there was no way I needed surgery. Again, the *Wonder Woman Denial Cape*... (Maybe I *did* actually hit my head while crashing down those stairs!)

Several days later I received a call from the hospital, telling me to be there the next morning for surgery. Again, I argued and stated that there was a mistake because no surgeon had called me about this. The nurse insisted that she had the right person and to be there. Steam was rolling out of my ears! I could not believe that this was happening: there was a mistake somewhere along the line, miscommunication of sorts! Wrong patient! Things slowly got worse for the stubborn me.

Will she have surgery or not? I have heard it said that if you do not listen to your body when it is telling you to slow down, either your body or the universe will ensure that you do! I went into this slow-down phase, kicking and screaming all the way. LOL

Now, my body and surgery (mainly the anesthetic) do not mix well. My blood pressure rises and my body goes into the "fight-or-flight" mode. It fights the anesthetic and refuses to calm down. As I go under, my body is fighting and it is still fighting when I come out of anesthetic. I also react badly to any type of pain medication that has a narcotic in it: I start hallucinating, vibrating with sweat pouring off my face, and vertigo and dizziness set in. At times, I can barely move due to the reactions I am having.

Therefore, the idea of having to go under for surgery was not appealing in the least! As I was waiting for the operating room to be ready, the anesthesiologist came over and talked to me about my two options for anesthetic: I could have a spinal tap or the regular "going under." I asked him which was better and he smartly remarked, "The one that works." (Hmmm, so I am not that impressed with him already.) I replied back to him, 'If I am going to have you put a needle in my back then your attitude better-well change.'

Now that is calling the kettle black. LOL! Soon, I was in the operating room with my bare back exposed, waiting for the anesthesiologist to arrive. I wanted so badly to be *anywhere* else at that moment in time, but knew it would soon be over and I could go home in a few hours. I hung on to that thought as the doctor proceeded to put disinfectant on my spine. Before he was ready to insert the needle, with my head hanging down, I asked him if he was in a better mood and suggested that he had better not miss the mark. He laughing replied, 'Yes, I am.'

I was gently laid down on the table with my knee on a brace to hold my ankle in the air, when the anesthesiologist started to put in a needle in my hand. I turned to him and asked him what he was doing? I didn't understand why I need an IV bag when I had the spinal done. As he was explaining to me why, my arm was blowing up like a balloon and big white blotches were breaking out! He looked at me and asked, "Is this normal for you?" I looked at my arm and groggily replied, "No."

Quickly, he stopped the IV solution he was using. The next thing I remember was my whole leg being rammed around as they tried to get the broken bones in my ankle to fit back into place.

With the surgery now complete, I was in the recovery room watching the minutes on the clock slowly tick by, thinking to myself that soon I will blow this 'pop stand' and be home to continue working on whatever I was doing that was important, instead of being here. My body was still trying to fight off the anesthetic while the nurses periodically came over to check on me. With a huge sigh, all I could think of was, "This is over!" Little did I know that there was more, much more to come in my near future, regarding that dam ankle!

The Wonder Woman Denial Cape was not ready to be put away just yet!

#denial #notwonderwoman #brokenankle #slowdowntime #surgeryisnotmyfriend

Story 21

Am I build weird?

UGH! Surgery for my broken ankle is done and I can't wait to go home from the surgery. Apparently I needed seven screws and a plate to repair the broken ankle.

I guess I am not Wonder Woman after all and 'Yes' I guess I do need a bone density test.

I never liked having surgery. My body does not like having surgery and it fights it all the way. Losing consciousness and having no control throws up red flags for me and I go into flight or fight mode. Staying in the hospital is even worse, but thankfully this was a day surgery, and I will be going home soon... or so I thought.

I was wheeled to my room after a time in recovery, and the surgeon came in, with a smirk on his face. I guess my telling the anesthesiologist to get in a better mood before he put in the spinal needle in my back had created some humor. For me, I was dead serious regarding the whole thing.

I was anticipating the news that I was released, but instead he looked at me and said that since I couldn't tolerate painkillers of any kind, I would have to remain in hospital overnight for monitoring.

BAMMM! The news hit me like a ton of bricks, not unlike the fifty pound cast on my leg. Before I could protest this unfair decision, he streaked out of the room, chuckling as he left.

As I lay there fuming, I started to get severe abdominal pain. When the nurse came in, I asked her if it was normal after having a spinal tap.

She replied, "No, that is not normal." and continued to adjust the IV bag over my head. Suddenly, I was again gasping for air as my abdomen felt like someone was dragging a knife along the inside. My goodness! I felt like I was about to give birth again!

I don't care what anyone says about that; I remember all too clearly how that pain felt. For those of you who may not have given birth naturally, or you who are the opposite sex, think of it this way: you are trying to shove a watermelon through the eye of a needle, a very small needle head at that! Not much fun in the doing part.

Moving on...

With sweat beading on my forehead from the pain, the nurse said this very simple thing, "Maybe you have to pee!"

I replied through gritted teeth, "Now why would I have to pee? I made sure I didn't drink any water so I would not have to pee."

She looked at me and pointed up to the IV bag, and replied, "This is your second bag. So just let it go and the catheter will do the rest."

"What catheter? I don't have a catheter," I replied.

And I was right! I guess in the hustle and bustle in the OR, they forgot to put in a catheter! Lucky me. Seriously: lucky me!

Suddenly the nurse was running to grab the commode chair (aka 'PeePee' chair) and after positioning it by my bed, she ran around to the other side and grabbed my IV pole. Finally, she assisted me out of bed so that I could "give birth" to the release of my very full bladder. Unfortunately, once my body shifted, several things happened.

#1. There was no holding back the tidal wave and

#2. It became obvious that there was no pan attached to the bottom of this 'PeePee' chair!

So, running me to the bathroom with my left leg sticking straight out like a guiding rod, and the IV pole crammed between my legs was a rather moot point since I was leaving a trail of evidence in my wake!

I am not sure if this is the same for other folks, but when my bladder is so full that it is ready to burst, for some reason only a certain amount of liquid is allowed to escape due to the pressure. Is there a valve in there, controlling the outpour, or am I just build weird?

As I sat there, perched high above the porcelain throne in my 'PeePee' chair, watching the nurse change the padding on my bed, I mused at the fact that I didn't care that I just peed my bed and all over the floor. Smugly, I thought to myself: "That will fix them, keeping me here over night!" OK, I admit this was not a nice thought for the poor nurse, but I was not in my right frame of mind, I think.

Drugs and I do not mix well; I will leave it there on that subject.

A few minutes later, the nurse came back to wheel me back to my bed. I was about to stand up and turn around when she gave out a shriek,

"Don't do that! I must help you as you cannot put *any* weight on your leg!"

Once I was settled back into my bed, and the nurse gone, the bladder attack came again! I buzzed the nurse, and together we headed off to the bathroom, IV pole and all. Again I peed the bed and left a trail behind me! Once again, the nurse had to change the padding and mop up the floor. When this happened again several more times, I finally decided that I could do this on my own when my bladder decided it needed emptying, which was often. They must have given me more than two IV bags, surely.

I had been nicely settled back in my bed for about 10 minutes when my bladder was making its voice heard. The only problem I had was that the 'PeePee' chair was by the door and not near enough that I could grab it.

Not wanting to attract any attention, I waited for a passerby, and asked if he could bring me the 'PeePee' chair.

Ahhh, freedom! I quickly positioned myself to swing into the chair and worked at maneuvering it to the bathroom, but the chair would not move. Damned I realized that the back wheel was locked.

So, here I was, trying with all might to drag this stubborn chair to the bathroom, with one leg sticking straight-out like some sort of guiding tool, similar to a Narwhal whale with its big tusk out front of its head. With my other leg on the floor I was gripping the floor with my toes, heaving the chair along my bed with the IV pole in between my legs, pulling on the bed-frame corner until the bed frame decided to join us on our journey to the said bathroom. At least this time I was not dribbling as I went!

Suddenly, I heard a yell (or more like a hard shriek…). "Mother! What are you doing?"

I looked over and saw my daughter, Martina, standing in the doorway. I was not sure what the look was on her face: Disbelief? Horror? Humor? Something else entirely?

Not missing a beat, I replied, "Will you help me get this damn chair into the bathroom?"

Without missing a beat either, she demanded, "Oh my god, why did you not call the nurse?"

"Because she has other things to do besides taking me to the bathroom every five fricking minutes." I answered.

It was a long night of many, many bathroom visits. By morning I was exhausted and ready to leave, but no.

"Wait! You now need a shower." Oh man, was this ever going to end?

So now I was in the shower in my favorite 'PeePee' chair, but minus the IV pole. Thank heavens for that improvement!

Maybe I should take this PeePee chair home with me, we seem to be rather attached to each other, I mused as I sat there with water flowing all over me.

With strict instructions to wait for the attendant to come and get me from the shower, I waited and waited. Patience is not my middle name, and soon I was doing The GREAT Escape down the long hospital corridor, trying to find my room. I had figured out by this time to push the chair backwards instead of trying to turn my toes into monkey-hands to crawl forward.

Finally, I found my room and was settled back into bed again, waiting patiently for the doctor to release me. An hour later the attendant found me. He was a bit surprised that I was here, as he had been searching all over the floor looking for me!

What can I say: can't keep a stubborn woman down?

Finally, the physio lady came and my crutches lesson began. I don't think they wanted to see me back again, so they made sure I was good to go when I was released.

All in all, I was not that bad of a patient. I was polite and courteous to everyone, except maybe the anesthesiologist, but he deserved that. Even though they tried to help me, in the end I just needed to be able to have some control back over the situation I found myself in.

#poor nurses #gottapeenow

Story 22

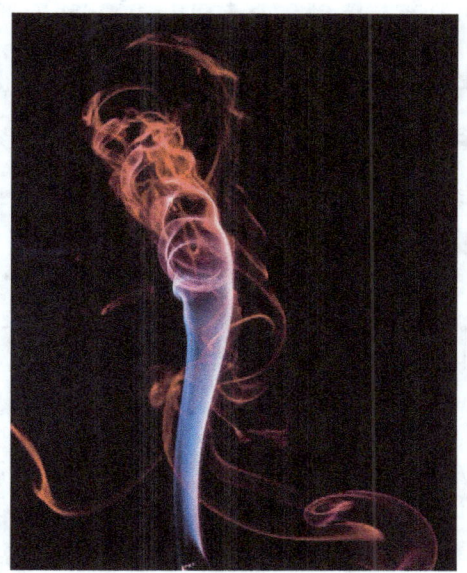

I am not helpless, I can do it!

Breaking one's ankle, then having surgery to repair the damage is never ideal. Even worse, this happened to me just in time for Christmas! To enable me to get around, we purchased a knee-scooter since my leg was to be non-weight-bearing for eight weeks. Adjusting to being mobile with a scooter took some serious new learning. I once flipped the scooter by turning a corner too sharply, and went over the handlebars a few times! I am sure my spirit-guides and angels just stood there, shaking their heads at this head-strong woman, struggling to come to terms with my new reality: "It is not in my control." I needed to allow myself to accept help now, as even my futile attempts of self-care suddenly depended on someone else!

Asking for assistance was foreign and difficult for me, as early in my life I had to learn to depend only on myself. I had recently begun to deal with a lot of horrible events from my past, one step at a time, and on my own terms. After a lifetime of running from danger, my instinct is to always be ready to escape. Now, suddenly, the inability to move quickly and freely was un-settling.

In spite of my mobility issues, Christmas was here and we had friends and family arriving for dinner. I have always single-handedly cooked the Christmas turkey and made the stuffing. However, this year Bud was excited to finally have *his* chance to do it instead! Moving around in our kitchen with the knee scooter was a challenge, so I was delegated to making the gravy. Whoopee!

Once the turkey was done and the potatoes cooked, all I needed was the turkey juice to add to the potato water to create my gravy. Everyone was milling around, chatting and visiting, waiting for the feast to be served. Bud had put the 30-pound turkey in a tin-foil turkey pan instead of our usual heavy roasting pan. I think that in his excitement of being in charge of cooking, he had neglected to put a cookie sheet under the foil pan before it went into the oven. (this way, you pick up the cookie sheet and not the flimsy tin-foil pan.) So, as Bud tried to lift the cooked turkey and all its juices out of the oven, the foil pan suddenly folded in towards the turkey, creating a funnel at the end, and spilling half of its juices onto the bottom of the oven! The result was a billowing pile of smoke! Immediately, everyone was waving tea towels around the wailing smoke detectors in an effort to get them to shut off! Seconds later, the alarm system went off, and the alarm monitor (mounted on the living room wall) had a lady asking if everything was ok! I told her, "Yes, there was nothing to worry about."

Once everything had calmed down, minus all the smoke in the house, it was finally my turn to make the gravy! I wheeled up to the stove and proceeded to start cooking. After a while, I noticed that the gravy was not thickening, so I wheeled forward to the pantry for some cornstarch or flour to thicken it. But while I was searching, the watery gravy boiled over onto the stove, and all hell broke loose again!

I could not move the scooter backwards; the back wheel was jammed into the cupboard! Now, smoke was absolutely *wafting* again from all the grease in the gravy, smoke alarms were screaming at full blast, everyone was running around, and no one could get to the stove because the back end of my scooter was jammed in the way! Suddenly, that lady from the alarm system in the wall was yelling, dogs were howling and barking over the high shrill of the detectors, and everyone was yelling and waving tea towels to stop the smoke detectors screeching! Bud was running around, opening windows to let the smoke out, so now cold winter air was blasting in, blowing across the kitchen to the table where all the hot food was laid out for our Christmas feast!

The furnace's air cleaner was turned on along with the oven fan, and amid all this bedlam, the lady in the wall continued to scream to be noticed! Miraculously through all the noise I heard her yell that the fire department had been dispatched! I finally wrestled the scooter free and skittered over to the living room alarm system, advising the lady that all was well, so cancel the Fire Department! Worried that these fellows would have to leave their own family Christmas dinners for a false alarm, I assured her that all was fine now, and she suggested that maybe they would put our system on a 12 hours lockdown in case another false alarm happened again. I agreed.

Bud managed to get the gravy off the hot burner. As the smoke cleared out of the house, I finished the gravy and we all sat down to enjoy our fine Christmas meal! However, with the open windows, what was once a *hot* Christmas spread was now cold, but at least everyone could heat up their food with the now-hot gravy! Suddenly, as gravy was being poured over someone's (now cool) potatoes, the gravy boat's lid popped off, and every ounce of that wonderful gravy gushed out all over the table!

Was this gong show ever going to end?

I am sure that this was a Christmas feast none of us will forget anytime soon! Through it all, though, we were grateful to be together and safe, and we finally enjoyed an evening of excitement and laughter.

The following morning I decided that the oven needed to be cleaned, so I proceeded by turning on the self-cleaning oven control. Within minutes, due to last night's spill, a small fire started in the oven. Once again, smoke began billowing out through the oven's venting system. This was not going to be a good day, I thought to myself.

I quickly turned off the self-cleaning mode, frantically waving tea towels to clear enough smoke to shut off the wailing smoke detector! As I was waving the towels, the lady in the wall once again came on, asking if everything was OK. Chokingly, I replied that I had tried to use the self-cleaning option on the oven but started a fire within it instead. It was out. And yes, everything was good, thanks.

Once the oven cooled down, out came the putty knife and the arduous task of cleaning the oven began. In reality it should have been Bud cleaning the oven, not me, but I was not sure if he would clean the oven the way I wanted it cleaned. So with my ice cream bucket of hot water, Scott towels and the putty knife, I went to work scraping away the thick layer of melted-on grease.

I hope to not hear from the 'lady in the wall' for a long while! Here's hoping.

So, How was your Christmas?

#noscootersinthekitchen #christmasorbust #memoriescreated

Story 23

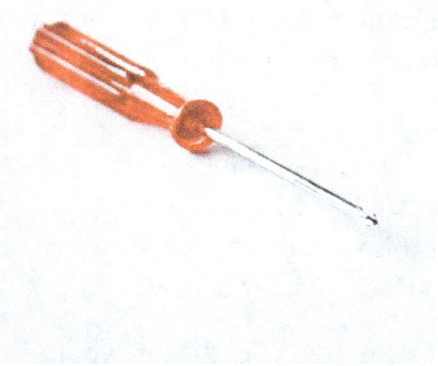

You're Kidding Right?

Six weeks had passed since my ankle surgery and it was time for a check up to see how things were progressing and to have the seventh screw removed.

On the two-week checkup, the surgeon told Bud and I that the seventh screw would have to be removed for it was holding my fibula (outside bone) and the tibia (inside bone) stable. While doing this, the screw was stopping me from being able to flex my ankle, which would probably break when I started riding again, due to the torque and pressure on the ankle. In light of this news I was not happy and asked him why on earth he would put in a screw that could break.

He said, "I put it in to stabilize the break." But if I decided to leave the screw in, then if the screw did break in the middle, I would have to have surgery again to it get it out. He would have to re-break my fibula to order to do that. Then he said that he could remove it in his office or in the operating room when the time came. I said that I was not having another surgery and he could remove it in his office.

So here we were, Bud and I, at the six-week mark, in the waiting room for the surgeon to come in and examine my ankle and remove the screw.

After our waiting about 30 minutes, the surgeon came in and looked at the ankle. I asked him if he was going to take out the 7th screw in ankle on this visit. He looked at me in utter confusion and said, "Why would I take out the screw?"

I answered, "Because you said that it would break and I would have to have surgery again."

"I have never removed a screw from a plate," he replied.

I looked at Bud and said, "Am I mistaken, or did he not say that on our last visit the screw must come out because it would eventually break?"

Bud replied, "Yes, you said the screw has to come out."

Still a bit confused, he said, "Ok, I will schedule the surgery."

I looked at him and said, "No, you said you could do it here in your office. I am not having surgery again."

He responded, "Ok, I will get my medical instruments, along with a nurse to help in assisting to remove it."

10 minutes later he arrived back in my cubicle along with a nurse. As I sat there he brought out this big, thick, 2 inch (5cm) long needle; I mean a big needle, the kind you would use on horses to get through their tough hide. My eyes were bugging out of my head as I looked at Bud, and swallowed hard. OMG!

There was no backing out now. The only consolation I had was knowing that within 30 minutes I would be done. I would not be in the hospital waiting for surgery, and then in a recovery room, waiting to go home hours later. I would not be taking up a bed and surgery room from someone else who needed it far more than I did.

I thought to myself, you got this girl!

The surgeon told me to lay down on my side and to hold still, and if I needed to I could scream, because he had hockey players and football players having this done and they certainly were doing a lot of screaming.

I swallowed hard and nodded my head and said through gritting teeth, "I will not be screaming!" As that first needle went in with the freezing compound, all I could get out without screaming was "Mary Mother of Christ,' that hurts! I started doing the child labor breathing exercise to stay still. It is amazing what one remembers to do. I gave birth well over thirty years ago to my twin daughters, and that breathing technique was right there.

Six injections later, I wiped the sweat off my forehead and laid my head on my arms, slowly breathing in calming down my racing heart.

After a few minutes, letting the freezing work, the surgeon whipped out the extraction tool to remove the screw. Proudly, he displayed his Mastercraft Philips hand screwdriver.

He explained that a power drill might work, but he wanted to take out the screw nice and slow. Extracting the screw was not that easy as he reefed and pressed on the ankle. Finally, the offending 2 inch (5 cm) long screw was out. Laughingly he asked, "Do you want to keep it?"

I looked at the screw with my bone marrow stuck in the grooves and bits of flesh hanging there and declined his offer.

With my leg re-stitched, bandaged, and in the walking cast, I was ready to leave. But I soon found out that walking out was a bit of a struggle because to my body once again was in that *fight or flight* mode. Bud quickly grabbed a wheel chair, settled me into it and wheeled me out!

It took several hours before I could get my body to stop shaking, probably due to the adrenalin still coursing through my veins. My instructions were: no walking on the ankle, no weight bearing, and no baths! (In two weeks we were due to leave for Mexico....this should be fun.)

Two weeks passed, and it was time for the stitches get to come out. Once more, I was in a cubicle at the Misericordia hospital, waiting for the surgeon to see my ankle.

After a brief inspection he told the nurse to remove the three stitches he had put in. Try as she might, she could not get the stitches out, so went to retrieve the surgeon. Try as he might, he was unable to remove the blue plastic stitches. Because the skin had grown over them, I was once again gritting my teeth through the pain of the scalpel cutting and scraping my skin, blood *pouring* down my ankle and soaking into the gurney's sheets! Finally, the surgeon decided that these stitches would have to stay in.

I let out the air I was holding and looked at my ankle, where the three blue stitches were still clearly visible through the skin. Apparently the knots had moved down inside the suture holes and were not willing to come out.

My daughters had always said I needed a tattoo, so this is it, tattoo stitches. LOL

Just before leaving his office, I asked the surgeon when I could start walking. He replied that he did not want me doing any weight-bearing yet. Seriously, it had been eight weeks already! I looked at him and said, "I leave for Mexico tomorrow."

Begrudgingly, he said, "Ok, a little weight bearing." Hallelujah!

Now came the moment of decision: should I take my knee scooter or crutches to Mexico? If I were to take the knee scooter, I could possibly flip, it or accidentally end up in the swimming pool with it, due to the inclines of the many walking paths in and around the resort. In the end, I opted for the crutches, as they would be safer: I did not need another broken limb! LOL

#mastercraftscrewerhasmanyuses #bestillmybeatingheart
#ihopetoneverdothatagain

#wonderwomanornot #mexicohereicome

Story 24

Draggin Behind

The difference between airports, and how they manage to help those in need, is astounding!

We had just arrived in Mexico from Alberta. Leaving behind the January snow and cold, Bud and I could not wait to feel some heat! Ahhh, the warm weather and sunshine would greet us once we were through the Mexican airport security.

I had prearranged for a wheelchair to greet me at the gate when we landed. I knew that trying to navigate customs and security was going to be very difficult with the cast on my leg, and the marching orders from my surgeon were, "NO WEIGHT YET!" Who knew that a silly broken ankle would take so long to heal!

We had friends and family who had travelled with us on this trip: Bud's son and his wife and their two children, along with Doug and Doris, good friends of ours.

Bud and I had just gotten off the plane when a young Mexican man approached me with the wheelchair. He asked if I spoke any Spanish and I replied, "No, Española, English." He laid my crutches over the tops of my legs, resting on the armrests, creating a space of four feet around me. Once settled, he proceeded to jog off, pushing me up the ramp into the airport section where our luggage was going to be ready for pickup.

Since I was carrying both of our passports and declaration forms, Bud had to run to stay with us. Now, Bud is a slow walker: he tells me it is because his legs are short, but I am not so sure! As we were whipping through all the other people working their way to Customs and security, I was trying to tell my attendant that we needed to slow down so that my husband could keep up. It was a relief to finally stop at the baggage carousel. Bud was puffing and huffing, but managed to stay close enough behind us. I figured for a guy in his late sixties, he was doing pretty good, but should actually do a little exercise to stay in shape. I certainly was not going to tell him that though.

Meanwhile, our family and friends were still getting off the airplane.

Our young Mexican chap was very eager to secure our luggage, and once we had our three large suitcases and my carry-on sitting on my lap, we were off again. Unfortunately, Bud was left struggling with the three large suitcases as once again we cut-off and weaved among the other travellers. At one time, we lost him in the crowd as people cut him off, and he was several people behind us. I was trying to get the young man (who had the energy of the Energizer Bunny!) to slow down and wait, but I must say that this guy was undaunted in his mission! Luckily, he whipped me into the Handicapped line and Bud, now behind us, managed to catch up as the security guys were scanning the wheelchairs in front of me. Huffing and puffing like a chain smoker, and with sweat running down his face, he was not looking too well!

Once we were finished with the last step in the Mexico customs, I looked to see if we could see anyone from our plane, especially our guests, but no one was even in sight yet! Off we went again, Bud dragging the suitcases and on the point of collapsing by the time we neared the exit, while I was a lady of leisure in my wheelchair! Out the door, we went directly to the tour-bus that would take all of us to the Hard Rock in Nuevo Vallarta. Thankfully, our tour director, Garth, helped Bud load the suitcases onto the bus. Finally done, Bud grabbed a bottle of water and went back to the exit area to wait for the rest of our crew. He needed to make sure that they all got on *our* bus, as there were dozens of big coach buses also parked there, waiting for their passengers.

Now, sitting on the bus, enjoying a cool bottle of water while I waited for the friends and family, I was so surprised that we had come off the plane, grabbed luggage and were through customs all within 20 minutes!

I must say that our return home and the adventures at the Vancouver Airport were not as accommodating!

During the flight from Mexico, we became aware that the attendant had checked-in Bud's son under Bud's name by mistake. This was an easy error as they both have the same initials and last name. No one until now had noticed the discrepancy, but consequently Bud's luggage was set to go to Kelowna and not Edmonton!

The flight attendant informed us that in order to get it all straightened out, we had to hike from the International Terminal to the Connecting\Domestic Terminal to get Bud's ticket and luggage tags changed in order to catch our plane to Edmonton. OK, that did not sound too bad.

Now, the Vancouver Airport is huge, and with no wheelchair or golf cart service, we had to drag our entire luggage over a mile through the airport! That was grueling! Due to the late hour of our arrival, nearly everything was closed and there were no attendants around. It was like we were walking in a huge deserted building that went on forever, up and down escalators, elevators and stairs. When we finally made it the Domestic Terminal, we had to navigate escalators and *more* stairs to find someone to help us with the ticket error. By the time we found someone to change the ticket, we only had about fifteen minutes to get to our plane, and we still had to clear security again!

Thank goodness Doug and Doris had stayed with us to help with our luggage, for I am not sure Bud and I would have made it that far. My armpits were rubbed raw by the crutches and from dragging my carry-on and various bags with goodies. Bud was still struggling with the other three large bags... (A tip and a word of advice: buy suitcases with the same kind of wheels that all move in the same direction, making life a bit easier and saving your husband from having a near heart attack!)

As they were calling everyone on our flight to prepare to board, I asked the security person if there was any way someone could give us a lift to the correct terminal. She replied, "Oh, it is only a five minute walk from here." I countered, "There is no way we are going to make it after the last mile we put in! Please get us a ride in one of the golf carts." She then looked at me with a grim smile (you know the ones, with the teeth clenched) and pointed to a bench and said, "A cart will be here soon." I think my tongue was hanging out on the ground by this time. Within a few minutes, a golf cart pulled up and the driver exited the vehicle. I thought, "Oh no, wait! Come back!" Thankfully, the security person motioned to us. The driver came back and helped load our luggage *and us* onto the golf cart. Away we went, wind whipping through our hair and drying off all the sweat we had running off our bodies. (By the way, it was about a 7-minute ride in the golf cart, so it would certainly have been a much longer walk!) We arrived just in time to be whisked down the runway and onto the plane.

What an experience, one I care not to repeat.

#airports #travellingwithbrokenlimb

Story 25

What the hell was I thinking?

Sometimes, great ideas are formed by bored minds, at least that is the case with me.

I was at a **Women Talk** event, and the Director from the Edmonton Dream Center was speaking about the Skydiving fundraising-event they were having. They were looking for people or companies to raise money for the Dream Center by skydiving. You had to raise a minimum amount of $2,500 in order to be able to jump.

So here I was, thinking that it was a great idea: I could help abused and/or victimized women to have to safe place to go, something that I knew I wished I had had when I was on the run from my ex-husband years back.

Right then and there I decided, "Hell yeah, I will do this!" and before leaving that evening, I had signed up to skydive and raise money. When I got home, I told Bud what I was doing, and he just shook his head with a smile on his face. I guess he knows me. LOL!

A few days later, I was telling my daughters, Martina and Tannis, what I was doing and they both decided they wanted to do it also. WOW! I was stunned that they wanted to do this amazing, crazy thing with me!

As the months went by, all three of us collected over the amount required to jump, and now we just had to wait for "jump day" to come in June.

D-Day finally arrived, and so far, I was still not nervous about jumping, just reserved, matter-of-fact-like thinking. Tannis, on the other hand was scared to death, while Martina was gung-ho to go! I paid to have videos of each of us during our jumps, as this was going to be something to remember and possibly something we may or may not do again!

The three of us were standing in the change-room being outfitted with our gear and partnered-up with an experienced skydiver. As we were standing there chatting, a CTV news reporter was filming us. He heard Martina jokingly tell her sister that she was going to shove her out of the plane. She knew Tannis was really nervous about jumping and was working at lightening up the tension. At least I hope so! LOL! He turned to me and asked; "Are you all together?" I replied, "Yes, these two ladies are my daughters."

He then asked, "Why are you jumping?" I explained that I was supporting the Edmonton Dream Center because I could have used a place like that when I needed it, and my daughters decided to jump with me to support the cause. He then asked, "Will you go outside so I can get a few shots of you guys with the plane in the background?"

"Sure" I replied. Off we went, thinking Holy-moly this is great, maybe we will be on TV!

It was not long before we had a few other skydivers who wanted in on the photo-op, but the news reporter was persistent in only wanting us three as part of his feature angle for the news story.

Once the photo was done, we headed back into the change room where we received further instructions on what was about to happen, and how we were to assist the attached skydiver. We were instructed that when it was our time to jump, we were to hold our arms across our chest and bend our knees, and when we landed we had to raise our legs so that we landed smoothly.

Next, off we went to board the small airplane that was going to whisk us up to 14,500 feet. I soon realized that I, being helpful, did not actually help myself when I had changed my jumping pants with another lady who could not find any to fit her. The new pants I had on did not allow me to raise my legs much. Trying to get my legs to bend enough to step on the ladder to the plane in the tight pants was not easy as I worked at climbing into the aircraft. Well, that was a feat in itself but I finally made it! Next, we were all shuffled onto a narrow bench and then strapped to our assigned skydiver. Martina was seated across from me and Tannis was seated behind Martina. There was not much room in the narrow plane as we huddled together, ready for takeoff.

Down the runway we roared and up we went! The sound of the plane was deafening as we climbed higher and higher into the sky. It does take a while to get that high and as we climbed Tannis had a hold of my arm in absolute terror. Boy, was I going to have a good bruise!

Now it was time to jump. I was still ok about what I was doing, but the minute I watched Martina go flying out the door into the abyss, terror struck my heart. Oh shit, what am I doing?

Without any notice, my sky driver was pushing me forward towards that gaping door. As I was perched on the edge of the plane, all I could say was, "Oh god, oh god" as I looked down at the far-away ground! Suddenly I catapulted into the wide-open space, flipping head over head plummeting towards the earth. My stomach was in my mouth and I thought I was going to hurl. Thankfully, we leveled out and now I was facing the earth, rapidly speeding towards me as we descended at over 100 mph per hour! No, that is miles not kilometres!

We were traveling so fast it was almost impossible to breath, and my cheeks were flapping like a chicken flapping it wings. Thank goodness for the goggles we had, for you would not be able to keep your eyes open without them. During this rapid fall, the skydiver was motioning me to look at the camera and smile (like I was having fun) for a picture!

We seemed to fall for a very long time and I was starting to get worried that my parachute was not opening when suddenly, BAM. It felt like my boobs were being pushed up through the top of my head and my legs were ripped apart as the main chute opened to slow our rapid descent towards earth. "Holy Mary Mother of God" that hurts. I was for sure going to have bruises now! In the back of my mind, I was thinking that maybe the pants ripped in that sudden tearing of the upper thighs so I would be able to land gracefully.

As we slowed our descent, I looked around for each of the girls, and was relieved to see both with their parachutes open.

To be that high in the sky and falling was both exhilarating and terrifying. I knew right then that this wasn't something I would do again. Good thing I have it on video! LOL

As we approached our landing point, my skydiver said. "Lift your legs". I tried to lift my legs. "Damn!" I replied, "I can't: the pants are still too tight." He countered, "If you don't lift your legs then you will break both of them in the landing." Oh shit, was all I could think of. I had seconds to figure out something, broken legs were not on my agenda. So as we touched down, I threw out my hips to one side, swinging my legs up the other way in an effort to not break them. In doing so, my skydiver landed gracefully and I in turn landed right on top of him, squashing him like a little bug. Thankfully, my legs did not break, but I was not so sure about the skydiver I was sitting on as he laid on the ground. Slowly he unbuckled us and I got up and then helped him up. I think he might have needed a bit of a break to catch his breath after that landing!

As each of us landed, we gathered together laughing with relief that we made it down safely.

Bud was there to capture all of the memory on the camera. That night, as we were watching the news station, up came our story about a mother and her two daughters jumping out of the plane. I was surprised that the reporter had used parts of the video of me jumping out of the plane! He also managed to get me clearly mouthing, 'Oh shit.' as I was propelled out of the plane in freefall. LOL!

Tannis, myself and Martina

#crazythingswedone #motherdaughtertime #onceisenough #skydivingforcharity

#livingbytheseatofmypants #offmybucketlist

Story 26

What does self-care have to do with it?

Today I decided that I need to do a Self-Care day, after all, we are heading off on a trip to Miami, Florida, and I do not want to look like I have just escaped from the forest people.

Therefore, I started by getting lovely fake eyelashes for my rather short, natural ones.

(Note: my regular girl is just learning about multiple lashes connected to one lash, so was not quite ready for this experience). I explained to the young lady that since I am allergic to the glue, I would need to have gel-pads applied instead of the Scotch tape they use to hold down your lashes. She was very understanding and thoughtful about this problem I have.

We proceeded. I was excited about how I was going to look, trying not to notice the itching going on in and around my eyes. (Suck it up princess, I thought to myself.)

About one hour and forty minutes later: time for the big reveal! Upon raising my eyelids, rather stuck together with the glue that I am allergic to, my eyes protested a bit.

The young woman gently but forcefully pushed me back down on the table and started prying my eyes open. I was thinking to myself at this point "Vanity sucks".

A short time later, the big reveal: Ta-da! Wow! They looked really good! Ignoring the itching for now, I marveled at my new eyelashes, long, full and luscious.

I paid the bill and tipped her, as she was very good at her job, and my eyelashes looked really good. (Not her problem I have a crazy weird allergy)

Now I was off to my next self-care event, a pedicure and leg waxing.

I arrived and this young woman thought it would be best to start with the pedicure first. I complied. The leg massage was good and she noticed the forest growing on my legs. I smiled and mentioned that I heard it is better if the hair is longer for waxing. She smiled and nodded. Meanwhile, I could read her mind: maybe two inches is a bit too long. I could braid it and sell it as hair extensions, I thought to myself.

With freshly painted toenails, we headed off to wax the legs. It was time to remove my winter insulation, time to cut down the forest. Bud might like this when I am done, I thought. He will not be sleeping with gorilla legs tonight! Frisky time later?...

I/We realized that I was wearing leggings with a rather tight ankle, so how were we going to wax my legs, as I could not get my pants off due to the wet toenails! Hmmm, a dilemma!

I managed to succeed at getting my ankle-size cuffs up and over my knees so she could proceed. (Good thing I was not doing the whole leg!) Now, my knees were a bit larger than my ankles, so they felt like someone had them in a stranglehold after just a few minutes.

Meanwhile, she proceeded to apply the wax to my first leg. I was thinking she would apply one or two strokes then attach the linen strip and pull it off. Instead, she applied wax to the whole front of my leg then proceeded to apply the paper and rip away!

@#@*, I guess it has been awhile.

I must say the first two strips were not that bad, but as she went along all I could think about was the guy in the YouTube video having his armpits waxed. I feel your pain man, I feel your pain!

The young lady said, "Hmmm, your legs sure are cold and it is hard to get the wax off."

You think??? My legs were *blue* from poor circulation caused by my ankle cuffs strangling my knees! In addition, she was trying to do a 'Rip-out–the-whole-forest' in one mighty sweep'! I managed to keep my thoughts to myself, as she was holding the mighty wax stick and linen strip! I smiled and suggested, "Hmmm, maybe if we only did a few swipes of the glue then rip away, it might work better." I was thinking to myself... No Brazilian happening here! The price we pay for vanity. Lol

Well, with the fronts done, now it was time for the backs of my legs. Another dilemma: my toenails were still wet with lovely pink polish, and we don't want leg hairs hanging on them now, do we? (From hairy legs to hairy toenails, yes, citizens of Miami, I AM from Canada where it is so cold even our toenails grow hair!) We decided that it would be good if I got off the table and jumped back on onto my stomach. I proceeded to jump off, but the table was still high and I nearly fell on my butt, as I had no circulation in my legs!

The young lady lowered the table so I could get back on, but I had to hang my legs over the end so as not to wreck the toenails. Thank goodness, there is less hair on my calves. Apparently, I rub that hair off somehow. Why wax at all? I guess I could walk backwards wherever I go… Hmmm new trend possibly.

So now, my Self-care day was complete. My eyes looked like I had been on a weeklong bender, and I was walking with my leggings stuck to my legs in places because the glue was too hard to remove from my cold legs! Vanity sucks.

No frisky time, legs stuck together and blood-shot eyes. Next time, Bud Portwood, next time!

All in all, a good day. It is all perspective.

#selfcarehasaprice #vanity #livelifehairy

Story 27

Disney World or Bust

I received word that my book, "I AM" was a finalist in the International Readers Favorite Book Awards. To me, this was a disappointment. I wanted to get the gold medal, the pinnacle award. It did not even occur to me that getting this far in a sea of thousands of books from around the world was an achievement, until Jo kicked me in the butt. I guess that is what friends are for, to give you a smack as a wakeup call!

I was attending an event in Red Deere, which Jo was hosting, called "The Best Kept Secret to Success." I enjoyed these events as I always found some interesting nugget to take home and work on. The weekend event was over and Bud was there to pick me up. I was packing away my vendors table when Jo came over and asked if I was going to the awards ceremony in Miami for our books. She had won a bronze medal with her book called "Frock-Off Living Undisguised."

I said, "No, I have not planned on it, as I was only a finalist." Bam! Out came the *kick in the butt* from Jo, and the lecture on why I should be going, and how a finalist position is a BIG DEAL! Within minutes, I was heading to Miami the following month! As the three of us stood there chatting together, Jo looked at me and said, "Have you ever been to Disney World?" Wait. What? Disney World? I looked at Bud and he looked at me, and I looked at Jo with disbelief in my eyes. I grew up watching "The Wonderful World of Disney" but never dreamed that one day I would go there, especially in my late fifties!

Jo booked us into a four star hotel in Orlando, Florida. How bad can this be, really, a 4-star hotel *and* Disney world? The two of us were like kids in a candy store whenever we talked on the phone about the trip. *Excited* was not a word to accurately describe how Jo and I felt about this escapade, a journey to the biggest fantasy-world *ever*! Time whipped past, and soon I was on the airplane flying off to our great adventure!

We had coordinated our flights to arrive within 30 minutes of each other in Orlando, and then we planned to hire an Uber or taxi to our hotel. ! I was flying from Canada and Jo was flying in from Mexico, where she and Michael, her husband, were staying for the winter. What could possibly go wrong?

Our adventure began with Jo's airplane dying on the tarmac in Houston, Texas. After several hours of sitting in a hot plane that was stranded on the tarmac, their replacement arrived. Call this plane a flash-back-in-time: they must have pulled it out of the National Aviation Museum, for it came with all the bells and whistles of a bygone era, including ashtrays and an overhead compartment that only the Harlem Globe Trotters could reach! To Jo, being a hair over five feet tall, this was a challenge to say the least! Luckily, a nice fellow traveler took pity on Jo's short stature and helped her.

Meanwhile, I arrived in Orlando only find that Jo hadn't yet arrived! After a few text messages and miles of hiking the Orlando airport to find a cab, I arrived at our hotel, minus 90.00 dollars U.S. in carfare. I believe my cabbie did not really understand English, or he pretended not to. OK, how was I to know that most people in the lower state of Florida spoke Spanish? I am just a country girl who grew up in the northern part of Alberta. Definitely not a seasoned world traveler, I do not think travelling four hours to Edmonton from my hometown counts. However, here I was, in another country, in a state that is bilingual, riding down a freeway with a Jamaican driver who does not speak English and with no apparent idea of where we were going! Call that a confidence builder, LOL, but alas, I finally made it to our hotel about an hour later.

Now, apparently in Orlando a four star room does not get you very much in the way of comfort. Nevertheless, we were close to Disney World, and hey! One has to make sacrifices in life! After a long day of travelling, I decided that maybe I would lay down for a bit while waiting for Jo to arrive. The beds looked so inviting and welcoming, begging me to lie down and be caressed by the lovely sheets and pillows. So, I kicked off my shoes and headed to the nearest bed for that much needed rest.

As I lowered myself onto the bed, it began to protest the invasion. It creaked and groaned and as I sank down into the mattress, my body never stopped until my butt was nearly on the floor! So there I was, sandwiched in the angry bed with only my feet and head sticking out. After much struggling a whole lot of grunting, I managed to pull myself free from its clutches.

"Hmmm, I wonder if the other bed is as bad?" I thought. Cautiously, I attempted to sit on the other one. Once more, I was assaulted by the bed, but this time I jumped up and managed to beat-off its clutches!

I soon realized that there had to be a sort of negotiation with these beds. One almost had to spread wide, like a snow angel: the same position you do when on thin ice, trying to save a person. (Which, by the way I have never experienced!) Therefore, trial and error was the game here. I knew I had to master these beds before Jo arrived, otherwise she would be lost in the depths of her mattress, and I would have to go in and rescue her. Knowing Jo is not that tall, I realized if only *my* head and feet were showing, there would be nothing of my friend to grab ahold of and pull out! In essence, she would be swallowed alive! So, I stood there, giving the beds my evil eye, deciding how best to tangle these wild beasts, now lying in wait! Suddenly, I pounced and landed on the bed in a spread-eagle position! The bed bucked and rolled, trying to get its bedcover around me, but I held fast to the bed-beast and soon it settled down to just mildly groaning and creaking. As I lay there contemplating my feat, a thought struck me; all these beds needed was the coin operated vibrating machine. UGH!

The struggle with the beds had taken longer than I realized, for a few minutes later Jo arrived, exhausted from her fun trip with the ancient plane. I cautioned her about the beds, so she gingerly sat on hers. There was much groaning and creaking but her bed held true. Soon we were both bouncing up and down on the beds and laughing our heads off at all the noise we were creating! The more we bounced, the more we laughed! Soon hysterics set in and for the next week we never stopped laughing. Everything was funny, and if it wasn't we made it funny.

After all we are from Canada, Yea.

Laughter truly is the best medicine.

#hotlebedsarethebest #beingakidagain #nevertoooldtohavefun #innerchild #laughlikenooneiswatching #laughtercuresall

Story 28

My, what lovely ears you have!

Who can count time easily? Apparently two Northern girls cannot, which is a good thing, otherwise we would have missed so much fun.

The Pandora exhibit had opened up in Disney World and Jo and I were both game to see and experience it. We were so excited to finally be here! We had done several Facebook Live episodes, documenting our adventures to date for those at home. At times, during the Facebook Live events, people would stop and stare at us as if either we had three heads or we were somebody famous! They just could not figure out which it was. So, during one of the impromptu videos, I looked at the audience we had gathered and volunteered, "We're from Canada." I guess that explained it all, and from then on, whenever a crowd gathered I would repeat this statement, then Jo and I would laugh. We were certainly having a good time with it all, and we will be remembered at Disney World. LOL

Arriving at the Pandora gate inside the Animal Exhibition grounds, we encountered a very long line up. The clock at the entrance posted that the wait-time to enter the Pandora exhibit was now 180 minutes. Both Jo and I looked at the time and said "Hmmm, not that long- only an hour and a half, so into the line we went. When the hour and half had passed, we were only at the halfway point, but we were at the entrance of the big pavilion housing the exhibit. We both looked at each other and burst out laughing again. We just realized that the 180 min was in reality 3 *hours* waiting time! Finally, out of the hot sun, we decided to continue on this adventure. No turning back now!

To keep everyone entertained inside the pavilion, it was set up that you were entering Pandora's jungles. There were animals and sounds to keep everyone amused as we snail-crawled up the long and winding ramps. Finally, we arrived at the pinnacle point, The Laboratory, and entered with eyes as big as saucers! We were in the movie scene where they made the avatars, what a remarkable sight! Right in front of us was a huge 8-foot Avatar (I am old school, you figure out the meters) floating in a tank, along with all the equipment hooked to it to keep it alive. WOW, how real it all looked! After looking over everything and snapping lots of photos, we then were sent into another room to await our next instructions on what we were going to experience. Not sure what it was, but we were told it was great!

Next, we filed into a chamber where we were matched with our own Avatar. On the wall ahead of us, our own picture and the picture of our Avatar was displayed, then we were led into another chamber that was a weight chamber of sorts, where we were matched with our Mountain Banshees (Ikran). On the wall in front of us, our own Banshee's picture and the signal that we were matched appeared. Off to the next chamber. Here, on the wall, we were showed our Mountain Banshees. Below them were mini motorbikes of sorts, Banshee crotch-rockets. Once we were settled on the crotch-rockets, and in the correct position for flight, an apparatus gently pushed and squeezed us into place so that we would not fall off.

Just like in the movie, the Mountain Banshees had to accept us as their riders. Now astride our Mountain Banshees, we waited for the adventure to begin! Jo and I were side by side, the excitement on our faces clearly evident! I looked at Jo and said, "I am going to enjoy this and scream my head off! We are never going to see any of these people in the chamber with us again, so let's let loose!" Suddenly, the wall in front of us fell away and we were in the world of Pandora! To say it was breathtaking does not describe it. We were standing on a cliff; below us herds of animals were grazing by the ocean, birds were singing and flying about, and there was a hum in the air. You could taste the excitement! We both knew a great adventure was unfolding before us, and we both were ready to soar! Our Mountain Banshees quickly took us soaring through the sky and along the cliff face. Many other Mountain Banshees were still on the cliffs, and as we whipped past them, they screamed at us!

Suddenly, our Mountain Banshees swerved and we were diving and swirling towards the ocean, as I screamed in delight! Just before hitting the water, we turned upward as a giant Hammerhead Titanothere (sea serpent-like thing) jumped up to grab us with his gaping jaws and many rows of jagged teeth! I swear I could see his tonsils as we narrowly escaped those jaws.

I admit that at this point, I was both laughing *and* screaming, adrenaline kicking in! "Jaws" has nothing on this creature! Water and wind were spraying us as we flew under a waterfall, barely missing the cliff face! Jo and I were laughing and screaming at the same time- this was *exhilarating*! We then flew to the dizzying heights of the floating mountains and back down again, swerving and diving under fallen trees and vines, wind blowing in our faces as we ducked our heads so we did not hit the rocks above us. We swept along the ground surface, racing with the running herds of Thanatos, Tapirus and Strumbeasts. It felt like you could reach out and touch them! Once more, we were whisked away up into the sky, soaring along, weaving in and out of the flying mountains. Barely missing crashing into the hanging limbs, we were ducking and swerving on our Banshees.

Soon, too soon in fact, our Mountain Banshees landed back on the cliff face and it was time for us to leave.

WOW, what a wild ride: 3-D at its finest!

I could do this all day. I certainly want one of those Mountain Banshee of my very own. Imagine me, flying around our farm, scaring our horses and then whipping over the neighbors to probably get shot at as their Llamas and cattle stampeded. LOL! Oh, the fun I would have! On the other hand, maybe I would ride the Direhorse instead; go trail riding with friends, scaring their horses and anything else along the path. Ok, better not, my friends might not like me anymore. My imagination was on overload!

Ok, back to reality. Jo and I exited the building with our hair standing on end from the wind and water, again laughing beyond control.

People around were looking at us as if we were crazy, which we were! lol! Since we probably were never going to see these people again, we had decided to let our hair down, just be ourselves, and enjoy what life and this place had to offer! After cleaning ourselves up a bit with a brush and comb, we entered the gift shop. We tried on everything and anything, including the famous Avatar ears, which Jo did buy, and proudly wears whenever she has a chance! LOL.

Whoever said the Disney World is only for kids was wrong! Jo and I slipped back into our childhood selves; each released our inner child, and had the best time ever!

Live life while you can, and never deny that inner child who is waiting for you to come out and play!

#donttakelifetoserious #exploreyourinnerchild #pandorarocks #mywhatstrangeearsyouhave

Story 29

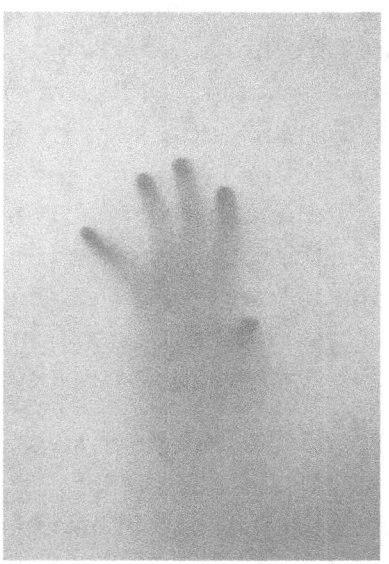

Apples and Trees

Before I even start this story, let me give you words of advice: DO NOT travel with your daughters and granddaughter if they are anything like you! You know the old saying: the apple does not fall far from the tree. Apparently, that is true! LOL

It was August and Marta, Martina, Tannis, Ahstyn and I had planned a few days away from everything- call it a Girls' Vacation! With my bestie, Marta, as our chauffeur we were heading to Radium Hot Springs via a route through Rocky Mountain House on Highway

11. Our first destination was the David Thompson Resort Motel, where we would spend the night and then head off the following morning all the way to Radium Hot Springs.

We arrived at the David Thompson Resort, hyped-up and hungry, looking forward to supper and an early night. Upon entering the parking lot, we came across a young person sprawled out on the pavement, apparently in distress. What had happened? Was it a hit and run? Did someone beat him up? Several people were milling around, trying to assist him, but he was having none of it as he lay there moaning. Marta and I went into the hotel office to check in, and asked the desk attendant what had happened. Apparently, while riding his bicycle, the young man tried to jump over the huge boulders blocking the entrance to the parking lot alongside the rooms. He miscalculated and landed on the concrete. Ouch! I hope that he is wiser for his experience with the pavement!

The desk attendant handed us our room keys, one for Marta and I and the other for the girls. Just before leaving the office, the desk attendant informed us that they did not have cell phone service and the Internet was down. Hmmm, I guessed we would pay-phoning home to let our husbands know we arrived ok. As there were no working phones in our rooms, the desk attendant pointed across the parking lot to the old phone booth. I was starting to feel like we were in the Twilight Zone! (Cue: the weird DooDooDoo music!) Opening the door to our room both Marta and I looked at each other and shuddered. This was not actually a "Resort- looking" room! In fact, it looked more like a room left over from the early 70's! There was a threadbare rug, stained comforters on the bed, cracked tiles around the discoloured sink, and the bathtub was even worse! You certainly would not even contemplate having a bath in it, and around the toilet area, there was hair on the floor. Gross!

Considering the age of the place, perhaps the room was as clean as it could be. To be sure, we DID NOT remove our shoes as we looked around. *My thought was: I think I will sleep just under the blanket and not in the sheets, if you please.* Although the room may have left something to be desired, the food in the restaurant across the parking lot was very good and the service was great.

The experience in the old-style phone booth was interesting! The operator informed us that only collect calls were allowed, and then apprised us of the cost per minute.

Ouch! The price per minute was an exorbitant amount so if I was too chatty with Bud, it could result in affecting our Jeep payment! I guessed it would have to be a very short chat. Let the good times roll.

The following morning, we piled into the SUV and headed off, having survived a night in the Twilight Zone.

Forest fires were burning out of control along the route we had chosen, so as we listened to the news on the radio we mapped out alternative routes to Radium Hot Springs. We ended up having to detour into the upper part of British Columbia via Golden and take highway 95. This added unavoidable time to our driving! To amuse ourselves we listened to tunes on the radio and attempted to play 'I Spy', but that did not fly really. We finally arrived at the Bighorn Meadows resort in Radium Hot Springs, where months ago I had reserved adjoining rooms for the five of us. We were definitely in for a shock. Our rooms turned out to be very small, each with one double bed and in separate buildings! Certainly not what we asked for. When we went back to the front desk to see what had happened, the lady informed me that they have foreign guests that sleep up to 8 per room, using the floor as a bed. I was shocked and replied, "Do we look like foreign guests that want to save money by sleeping on the floor? We have five in our party and each of us requires a bed, preferably in the same suite!" After much haggling, we were given a Condo suite with two bedrooms and a pullout couch in the living room.

As we all climbed up the stairs to the unit we again were in for a shock, but this time it was a pleasant one. This was someone's home, used for rental income when they were away! It was spacious and clean, included a washer, dryer, balcony, kitchen, dining room, living room and two bedrooms: one with a king bed the other with twin beds. Now *this* was more to our liking!

All of us relished several days of canoeing, stand-up paddle boarding, the hot springs, and floating down the river on tubes. We enjoyed walking around the gated resort and looking at the bighorn sheep that apparently lived on the golf course. The air was good, as the smoke from the fires ravaging the forest had blown our way. It was certainly peaceful, as many of the vacationers who would have been in Radium had decided not to come. There were no crowds to deal with and we had our pick of excursions to enjoy.

On the third night we were there, my girls decided that they needed to have a little bit of fun. We had all gone to bed. Marta and I were sharing the master bedroom with the ensuite. Both of us had stayed up working on puzzles or something on our iPads when finally we decided to hit the sheets. Marta was out like a light, but I was still restless and was dozing but not sleeping, watching the television. I was in this semi-sleep phase when I felt the sheets move on the bed! My eyes popped open in an instant and I laid there waiting… the dull glow from the television was giving off enough light that I could see without turning on the bed-side table lamp. I slowly scanned the room, searching for an apparition of sorts.

Once more, the sheets moved, and I rolled over and whispered to Marta, "Did you feel that?"

No reply.

What the hell? Is this place haunted? Seriously to God, no! Again, the sheets moved but this time with a bit more force. I slowly slipped out of bed and started to creep along the side of the bed towards the end. I was not sure what I was doing or what I expected to find, but I was going to find out what spirit was haunting me this time!

As I slowly came around the foot of the bed, I let out a scream! Lying on the floor was a white apparition! Marta jumped up in the bed at my scream, the door flew open and all hell broke loose! Lying on the floor, the white apparition was laughing hysterically, along with Tannis and Ahstyn who were now in our room, bent over, holding their sides and laughing out of control. Apparently, they had had a bird's-eye view of the whole show while standing in the hallway, peeking through the crack in the bedroom door! I think my heart had stopped there for a minute until I realized that *Martina* was the apparition as she slowly climbed up off the floor. Hysterically guffawing, she cried, "You should have seen the look on your face!" All I could say was, "You shits!" as I stood leaning on the bed, trying to slow my breathing. Marta, now fully awake, was also chuckling and soon there we were all laughing out of control together. Memories!

I was very impressed with how quiet the three of them had been order to pull it off. I am not sure how they managed to get the door open enough for Martina to slither through on her belly to the foot of the bed. I am guessing it was only because the whole condominium unit was blacker then the Ace of spades. Already I was planning of my revenge on the three of them!

I must say that for a long time after that, the three girls enjoyed their private memories of the night they scared the crap out of their mother! I think they aged me a few years with that one.

It was our last night in this rental, and payback time was fast approaching. With the Condo quiet and everyone in bed, now it was *my* turn to scare the heck out of *them*! Since they were not all sleeping in the same room, I decided to start by scaring Tannis and Ahstyn first while they were in that state of semi sleep. I opened their door and ran and jumped on the bed, roaring, then spun and ran out the door and into the living room to scare Martina! During this flight, I had to make sure I did not run into anything and kill myself! Tannis and Ahstyn were certainly scared, as Ahstyn was still screaming but now yelling "Grandma!" All the noise startled Martina, but not as much as I would have liked. Overall, payback was good. Marta was laughing as she came down the hallway, and soon the whole place was in an uproar!

Therefore, I again forewarn you about travelling with your adult children: if they are anything like you, life could get very interesting!

I look forward to the next trip with all of them!

#pranksters #threeamigosfortrouble #ghosts #paybacktime #memories

Tannis, Ahstyn and Martina

Marta

Story 30

Who on earth would Willingly to do this?

Once again, let me say that I am willing to do almost anything, and when our friend Doug wanted to go on the Tsunami boat ride, you guessed it: I was game! After all, how bad could it be: the water rolling over above us, as if we are inside of a giant tunnel wave!

We were back in Puerto Vallarta, Mexico, and Doug and Doris had come with us again. As we sat looking over the excursions available, one interesting one popped up called Tsunami. It was a huge jet boat that whipped around the bay, spinning 'U'ies in the water, taking off at top speed before slamming on the brakes to create a huge wave! It then repeats this, quickly spinning and slamming on the brakes several more times, then driving the nose of the boat into the water to allow the huge waves to roll over the boat, thus a Tsunami of sorts.

Now I am not big on ever having my head under water, but for some unknown reason I agreed, so the four of us were booked for the tour.

The following day we headed off to the nearby marina where the boat taxi would take us across the waterway to Vallarta Adventures. From there, we caught another boat and headed off to the adjoining bay where the Tsunami Boat tour office was. As we were not sure how long it would take to get to the Tsunami tour office, we had arrived early. With time to kill, time we had a few extra minutes to walk around the marina area, looking at the shops there. By now, the weather was very warm and we were starting to sweat a bit. The marina water looked so cool and inviting, but there was no way get down to it to dip your toes in.

Famished, we decided to go and grab a bite to eat at the Johnny Rocket restaurant situated along the dock. As we slipped into our 1950s booth, a young waiter approached and took our orders for hamburgers and fries. The fifties music was playing and the waiting staff were putting on a floorshow for the customers. It was fun joining in, clapping for them as they performed the fancy floorshow!

After lunch, we headed back to the office for **The Tsunami**, and given change rooms so that we could get into our bathing suits. They advised us not to take caps or sunglasses, as they would fly off our faces. When we came out of the change rooms we realized that we were going to be the only guests on the boat that held approximately 30 passengers. This was going to be fun! We walked along the dock area where I was a bit surprised to see a huge 12-foot crocodile laying in the water right below me! (Ok, now maybe I didn't want to get in the water *at any time* for *any reason!*)

We climbed into the boat where we were instructed to sit so that we had a bar in between every two people. I guess this was so you were not squashed during the ride; good thinking on their part.

Soon we were on our way out of the marina, passing the yachts docked there, and the big military boat that our guide told us was used to the patrol the waters. Leaving the marina, we entered into the large bay that surrounded the area. The minute we were clear of the entrance, our boat kicked into high gear and away we raced! Those big four outboard motors roared to life as we flew along the coast for about two miles! My hair was flying in the wind and the sun warmed my face as I enjoyed the speed of the boat and the views. Suddenly, the driver held up his arm and circled it in air. That was the cue that he was going into a spin, and into a spin we went! Water was spraying everywhere and the side of the boat was nearly parallel with the ocean water as we spun in a 180-degree circle! I was inches away from the ocean and I swear you could see fish scrambling out of the way. Just as fast as we went in to the spin, out we came again as the boat straightened and headed off again across the bay.

Yahoo- was that fun, and before long, we saw his cue once more and we were spinning in the other direction! Now I understood why the bars were in place on the seats, for without them I would certainly have ended up in the ocean when I crushed the people I was leaning on during the nearly horizontal spin on the ocean water.

We did several more spins before the driver was in the correct spot for the Tsunami. His teammate was on the shore waved his flag to start the Tsunami. Away we went, speeding and slamming on the brakes to start creating huge waves! When a significant amount of wave was achieved, the driver whipped the boat around yelling, "Duck and hold your breath!"

'Oh God, I think I am going to drown', was the only thought in my head as the sandy water pummelled us, ripping at our life vests. It felt like forever! Ok, I know forever is a long time, but for someone who hates having water over her head, it was an extremely long time! When the water finally subsided, we all looked like drowned rats with sand in our hair and in our bathing suits. None of us was interested in experiencing *that* again. Therefore, after a brief discussion and a consensus, we informed the driver that we were NOT interested in experiencing the bigger Tsunami that he was trying to sell us! Nope, no way not happening!

We told him that he certainly could whip around the bay doing his papa wheelies instead. Thank heavens there was no one else on board; otherwise we would have had to endure more Tsunamis. I think I might have strongly considered jumping overboard if that was the case.

With the ride over, we returned to the office and headed for the showers to try to remove all the sand from our bodies and hair! The attempts proved futile, as sand was caked into us!

Now, to our surprise, our newest discovery was that there was no ride back to the marina we had come from! What the heck? At length, with some difficulty due to language and our location, we did finally manage to get a cab to take this miserable, soaked, foursome back to our hotel to enjoy a warm shower and soap!

#someadventuresarenotsofun #drownedrats
#faketsunami #thrillingride

Story 31

How hard can it be? Dam hard.

To say I am an adventure-seeker might be a stretch, but on the other hand I do like to try different things to see if I like them. Scuba diving was one of those things that I thought, 'How hard can it be?'

We were back in Mexico, and during the past two years I had tried very hard to embrace snorkelling.

You see, I am terrified of drowning. I must have been a Viking in a past life because every time I am swimming, I start out like a normal person, kicking my feet and slowly navigating through the water. Soon my legs start to drop down, and before I know it I am vertical in the water and sinking like a Viking warrior wearing his full metal armour! Down, down I go, sinking with my ship. So to say that a life jacket is in my life is an understatement.

On this particular trip to Mexico some friends of ours, Doug and Doris, came with us and Doug decided that he wanted to go scuba diving. I was game, for I figured I could not really drown because I would have an oxygen tank strapped to me, so voila: I would be able to breathe even under water. I knew this was the solution to my fear of drowning.

So, bravely, Doug and I went and took a 30-minute orientation on how to scuba dive. The instructor was very adamant that if your face mask started to fill with water you must poke your forehead with the index finger, tilt your head back and blow, releasing the water. Now I am a very good student and I listened hard to his instruction: after all, I did not want to drown if at all possible.

Once orientation was complete, we trudged across the sand and towards the pier where we would get into the water. Trying to walk across deep sand with an extra 70 pounds strapped to your back is not so easy. I equate it to walking on hot burning coals in bare feet carrying ten watermelons. I was sure glad to finally make it to that pier!

At this point in time my knees were screaming at me, "What are you doing, trying to kill us?" Since I had torn meniscus in both knees and had not had my surgery as of yet, I guess they were protesting a bit much.

Soon, the instructor told us to step off the last step into the water where he would prepare our masks, mouth pieces and buoyance vests. Bravely, I stepped off the last step and sank about 20 feet (actually probably only 6 feet but still: water over my head is water over my head! I came flying out of the water like a banshee, eyes rolling in the back of my head like Linda Blair from The Exorcist, flailing my arms and spitting seawater from my mouth and nose.

After the instructor calmed me down he said, 'Why don't you try snorkelling over there, away from everyone else". Hmmm, I can't say what I thought, but it involved a few four letter words, but dutifully I did as he said.

Let me explain that trying to snorkel in scuba gear looks like a whale giving birth, you are forever rolling over and flopping everywhere. Not a pretty sight.

Try as I might, I just could not get the hang of it. Every time I tried to go down under the water (even a few feet my visor filled with water and I would hyperventilate. Meanwhile I was poking my frigging forehead which by now had a big red dent, and trying to blow out the water from my mask. Soon, very soon, I was breathing out through both my nose and mouth, when you are only to breathe out of your mouth ('Hmmm: fat chance on that one.' My body was in full panic-mode, survival of the fittest and I was losing the battle. With all the hyperventilating I was doing, I figured my air tank was depleting its oxygen supply pretty fast!

Below me I could see everyone swimming around the statues that sat on the bottom of the sea floor, getting their pictures taken and having a ball. Suddenly I saw Doug swimming past, enjoying himself, waving at me. If I wasn't busy holding my mouthpiece in my mouth to stop sea water from coming in, and poking my frigging forehead with my other hand, I might have flipped him the bird.

Alas, I decided that this was not going to work and looked around to see which way I had to swim to get back to shore. Suddenly, out of the mist came my rescuer!

As I watched this Mexican god swim toward me I was mesmerized by his smooth, fluid, arm stokes as he reached for me. Holding me in his strong arms, he so slowly lifted up my face mask and gently wiped my face.

Halt, wait, why are you wiping my face?

A light bulb blinked above my head and I realized that while hyperventilating through my mouth and nose, all the sea water had inadvertently cleaned out my sinuses! With any shred of modestly that I might have had now gone, I realized I had just used the world's largest Nettie-pot! When he had finished wiping all the stuff off my face, he looked at me and said, "Hola, my name is Fabio and I am going to help you." Relief flooded through my body. Finally I was getting out of this ocean and back to dry land.

After cleaning my mask with sea water, he quickly placed it back on my face and tightened it up so that my very short eyelashes were now flickering against the plastic eye piece. Then he grabbed hold of my hand (as the other one was still holding the mouthpiece in place) and down we went. At times I thought my head was going to explode and my inner right ear drum was ready to burst due to scar tissue and being deaf in that ear. Slowly we navigated down to the ocean floor, stopping every once in a while to regulate my air and ease the ripping pain in my head from descending. Once down on the floor, I looked up and nearly started to panic when I saw how far down I was, but quickly decided to look elsewhere.

So now where was that photographer to take my picture?

Hmmmm, nowhere to be found... figures!

Fabio and I swam around for a while, looking at the fish and statues on the sea floor. During this time he never let go of my hand. He led into the places where there were caves and reefs for the fish to live in, places that I knew I would never have seen without his help.

Soon it was time to surface and the scuba diving was over, thank God for that. As Fabio exited the water to head over to the orientation center, I noticed that this Fabio was about as wide as he was tall (which was not that tall) with flowing black hair! Certainly not the picture of Fabio we all have in our heads from those romance novels you see in the book stores. But one thing about this Fabio: he saved my butt in that ocean, so in my eyes he was that Mexican God!

In life, sometimes you lead, sometimes you follow, but rarely do we go through life without help from another. Thanks Fabio

#scubadivingbeginner #fabio #everyoneneedsahelpinghand

Story 32

Finding the Mini Cooper

Ever since Bud and I have been together, he often talked about the Austin Mini Cooper that he drove when he was younger. He loved that car, and hoped one day to get another one when we could afford it. I also had wanted a mini, but could never find one that needed a home.

One day, a miracle happened! I found a Mini and decided to surprise Bud with it as an early birthday present for him. I was so excited with the prospect, and I knew Bud would be shocked when it arrived; the anticipation was electrifying!

To share in our good fortune, I started posting hints on my Facebook page:

> *2016: Well, as Christmas approaches, I reflect on all the years of wish lists. Bud has always wanted another Mini, but the timing was never quite right, or something else got in the way. He would tell me about what he would do if he ever got a Mini, and I would listen patiently to his about his Wish-List ramblings. Now in the past two years with our economy not doing so well, the idea of getting him a Mini was nearly impossible. However, fate intervened, the universe shifted, and our new (slightly used) 2015 model is to arrive on Wednesday! I will post the picture of Bud with our (not solely his, after all; share and share alike) Mini on Wednesday. Stay tuned.... Bud will be so surprised!*
>
> *I should get the Wife of the Year Award for this one!*

The days seemed to drag by as I waited in anticipation for the mini to arrive. Since it was the beginning of winter, we had to make sure that there was a suitable place to put the Mini, one where it would be protected from the elements, yet have a space of its own so that we could marvel at its beauty.

Preparations were well in hand when the day finally arrived. I posted the exciting news on my Facebook page:

> *The Mini Cooper is on its way.*
>
> *Five speed, short wheel base, drives well, corners like a dream.*
>
> *Bud will be thrilled: one more thing off his wish list. Yeah! Pictures to follow.*

Now, I do not know about you, but when new and exciting things happen, I find that the waiting part is the hardest!

The Mini has arrived, and the look on Bud's face is priceless! To say that he was genuinely surprised is an understatement.

Is that a look of utter surprise?

Everyone: please let me introduce Miss Mini Cooper! She is a 2015 model, steel gray and comes with a very big attitude. By the way, Bud was in on the trick to everyone. LOL

2015-2019

Cooper turned out to be an escape artist, and with our post-and-rail fences there was <u>no</u> keeping her in! Just like the song, "Don't Fence Me In", that was her motto.

Cooper arrived with Tannis's rescue colt, LeRoy. Both were very young, Cooper about one and a half years old and LeRoy about six months. They had both been starved and were going through the Auction mart when they were purchased by an individual who wanted to save them. This person sent a picture of him to my daughter, Tannis, hoping she would be interested in buying, in the background stood Cooper. It was love a first sight for me, and soon both horses were purchased and coming home to our place! I don't know why Cooper was sold. Physically, there was nothing the matter with her, so maybe it was the fact that she was an escape artist! Alternatively, perhaps they did not have enough hay to feed their horses. Poor LeRoy! He was very skinny and had been born with a clubfoot, and Tannis was hoping to have it fixed. Neither of them were particularly interested in humans. I guess I could not blame them there. We had our work cut out for us to gain their trust.

On her first day here, Cooper decided that she was leaving. She slipped under that fence and took off, running across the field. When she realized that her buddy LeRoy was not following, (as he could not easily slip under the lower rail of the fence,) Cooper did a U-turn and headed back, ducking under the fence as we came around the corner! We had witnessed this great escape, but Cooper thought we had not and looked at us with those big brown eyes, all innocent. I knew at the moment that she and I were kindred souls!

In order to try to keep her in their pen, thus safe from harm by the larger horses, I tried running an electric wire along the bottom rail. When I came out the next day, the electric wire was strewn all over the ground, and again Cooper looked innocent! As spring came, Cooper was continually slipping under the fence and wandering all over the lawn area, enjoying the nice grass while the mares continued to call for her when she was out of sight. They certainly treated her like one of their foals and I believe she was definitely a novelty for them all. Hughie, my big guy who stood seventeen hands high, was in love with her; she became his person, his companion.

One day, I had not seen Cooper around and decided to see if she was ok, only to find her stuck with more of my electric fence wrapped up in her tail. How she managed that I don't know, as the electric wire was along the top railing of the fence, about four feet (1.3m) above her. I stood there laughing at the sight, shaking my head as I cut away all the wire and part of her tail, which needed trimming as it was dragging on the ground!

Eventually, Cooper realized that she was allowed to wander wherever she wanted. By now, escaping had become boring, so she decided to venture out of the far pasture and visit the neighbor's pasture. I was surprised to receive the neighbors' complaint one day that she was preventing their horses from coming when called! I hopped onto the gator and went looking for the culprit, only to find her in our pasture, peacefully eating. Hmmm. what is going on? I thought.

A few days later, another phone call came from the irate neighbors, and once more, I headed out to find Cooper, again she was in our pasture with our mares. Therefore, I decided to do a stakeout and watched from our house to see if she was indeed escaping. It did not take long for me to see her out in the field and sauntering towards the neighbor's fence line. Into the gator, I hopped and headed off. When Cooper saw me coming she turned and hightailed it as fast as she could back to the pasture! As she was squirting under the fence, my foot connected with her butt as the gator went past her, telling her, NO!

Something needed to be done! I called a friend of mine who can talk to animals. When Mary arrived a few days later, Cooper was in the back yard eating grass. When Mary was out of the vehicle, Cooper was there like a watchdog, sizing her up, deciding whether or not this person was truly allowed on the property. As Mary headed over towards the other horses where I was standing, Cooper stood and watched her, sizing her up. Suddenly, without warning, Cooper was in a gallop, heading straight for Mary, and rammed her in the butt with her head! I guess Cooper did not want to have her chit- chat with Mary, which surprised me. When both she and LeRoy came, we had Mary tell them that they were safe, and this was their "forever home".

With Cooper now in the barn, Mary tried to communicate with her. However, Cooper was not listening and fought the whole idea: she would not look at Mary, she would not stand still and she kept trying to leave. So, finally I sat down on a pail, held her face in my hands and told her the rules that she had to abide by if she was going to continue having her freedom. After that day, Cooper never left our property again. She stayed in her allowed areas, which included all of the pastures, even with the geldings if she wanted, and the whole yard area, which is quite large.

On many days, she and I would sit together in the warm sunshine on the lawn, discussing life or just enjoying each other's company. Soon, Cooper was given an alias: **Tina Turner,** due to her thick silver locks that refused to be tamed and always stood up at attention when she was running across the field. She was a force to be reckoned with.

Cooper was not like any other horse I have had. If II was in my work shed using the table saw, Cooper was in there with me, watching what I was doing. Wherever I went, Cooper followed. During pig roasts and birthdays we held at the farm, Cooper was the center of attention, checking out everyone and sampling all the desserts she managed to sneak. We all enjoyed her company and loved seeing her in the back yard, munching on grass. Amazingly, she never bothered with any of my flowers or the garden.

As we spent time together, I realized that Cooper was probably a mini-me in a horse's body as she certainly had more than a few of my traits. LOL

There were times when her stubborn streak would kick in and it was a battle of wills.

She is very much missed, as her existence in all of our lives made us better. I am happy to say that during her short life with us she had the run of the farm. We had adjusted a section of railing fence in each pasture so that she could easily get under, as she grew taller. There was nothing too good for our Miss Mini Cooper.

#minisaregreat #missher #bestminiever

Story 33

The Taco of Sorts!

Once more, Jo and I were heading off to another "Best Keep Secret" event she was hosting. This time we were heading to Red Deer, Alberta with an additional guest, Meghan. Since Jo and I had roomed together before we knew what we were in for. Megan, who was going to share our room to cut the cost, did not.

Once the event was all set up and supper was done, we headed off to our hotel room, where we noticed a queen-size bed and a rollout couch. We gave Megan the bed, as she was the driver. Jo and I were going to take the couch, but then we decided that maybe they could bring up a cot for Jo instead, since there was room enough to fit one.

I am not sure what it is with Jo and I, but all we have to do is look at each other and we are laughing! This time was no different: I think Megan thought we were crazy!

When the cot finally arrived, I proceeded to help get it set up, only to nearly crash through the fifth-floor window when the cot decided that it had a mind of its own! Upon seeing my dilemma, once more Jo and I were sharing uncontrollable laughter as we tried to wrestle the wayward cot! We should have clued in right then and there that this bed had a mind of its own, but we did not. (There must be something about Jo and I with wayward, miserable, life-sucking beds with minds of their own, as this was not the first time!

After wrestling the cot back into submission and in place, we were finally ready for bed. Megan was comfortable in the queen bed, all snug as a bug in a rug. My hide-a-bed should have stayed hiding, though, for there were loose springs sticking up in the most inappropriate places making it difficult to find a comfortable spot to lie. Finally, after much moving and bouncing around, I ended up lying across the bed sideways in an attempt to find that comfortable place.

Jo, on the other hand, was in far worse shape than I was! The minute she sat down on the bed and swung her feet up to recline, the bed attacked and swallowed her up! All you could hear was muffled laugher coming out of the folds of this giant taco that had eaten her. I crawled over to the end of my bed and again we were in hysterical laughter! The only visible parts of her were the tips of her toes and her nose; the rest was gone. Jo's butt was barely 2 inches off the floor as the springs in the cot quivered with the excitement of having a victim in its grips!

Megan, in the meantime, who did not get the two of us, insisted on telling us to quiet down, which only made us laugh more. Poor Megan was not going to get much sleep.

I asked Jo if she wanted help getting out of the bed, but she decided that since she was in it already she might as well stay there. She claimed that it was comfortable, but I think that was the bed giving off a subtle smell that rendered Jo unable to think clearly. She was at the mercy of the 'Taco Bed'.

The following morning I was not sure what I would find. Would there be any sign of Jo in the Taco Bed, or was she gone for good? How was I to explain this to her family? How was I to say, sorry but your mother was eaten last night by a Taco Bed? Oh, the plight of the situation!

I swallowed hard and bravely crawled over to the end of my spring-poking bed to see what fate awaited us. Slowly, I scanned the bed for any sign of Jo: was she still here with us? That was the question. I leaned forward a bit more and was with flooded with relief when I noticed a slight movement within the confining folds of the bed! Was that a hand breaking through to the surface? Yes, but I had to act quickly for Jo was still stuck inside the mouth of taco that still held her within it grips. I leaped from my bed like Wonder Woman, and with my two hands gripping Jo's I slowly started pulling her out of the Taco cot. With a sigh and a groan, the bed was slowly being forced to release Jo, embedded in its grips. Finally, I was able to extract my friend from the clutches of the cot in one piece. Thankfully, she survived the swallowing Taco Bed to rise and live another day.

So a word of caution: beware, very aware of hotel beds, for some of them surely are possessed and do not want to give up their victims without a fight.

#unrulelycots #tacoofsorts #noendtolaughter

Story 34

Double or Nothing!

Today was my 60th surprise birthday party and I was going to kick up my heels and have a ball! The July weather was great: not too hot, not too cold, and the pig was in the pig roaster cocking away. Marta and the girls were in the barn, secretly decorating it, and the food was all prepared for the fun to begin. In the mix of things was our mini, Cooper, enjoying all the attention she was receiving. Just before supper, she was in the barn with my daughter and granddaughter, helping herself to the snacks on the table: chips and Oreo cookies became her favorites!

Some of my cousins had come from afar to see and visit with my Dad, who had also managed to come. There were speeches given in my honor, and much to everyone's delight, Marta and Don climbed aboard our tractor and sang a duet, "Do You think My Tractors' Sexy?" Then the dancing began with a break for supper and then more dancing on the lawn, which was uneven. Everyone was having a blast as the DJ blasted out all of the old-time dancing tunes of the Rock-n-Roll era, with occasional requests thrown for Garth Brooks.

Ty loved to dance with me, so around the lawn he and I danced to Garth Brooks. Tukker was not inclined to twirl the floor; he is too much of an introvert dog! This was our first official party in what is called the 'Party Barn', and everyone was having fun! What originally started as a barn for my horses has never been a horse

or stall in it! It became something that we had never planned-for. Oh, horses were in it but only for vet care or tacking-up to go riding. Funny how life changes plans! The next morning, I was sure feeling all the dancing I had done: my knees were killing me, and for the next months I hobbled around with a very painful right knee feeling like someone was grating a knife across the insides.

Now it was November, and I was heading off to Miami, Florida, for the "Readers Favorite Books Awards", but first a quick and funny trip to Orlando and Disney World with Jo were in order! After the whirlwind trip to Disney we both flew off to Miami and all the excitement that awaited us there. Once more, we hit the ground running, me hobbling but refusing to allow my miserable right knee to slow me down. In one of our excursions we hit K-Mart and decided to try on every hat and onesie. Then we headed off to the dressing rooms to try on crazy clothes, like giant granny nightgowns while wearing tiaras and Jo's big glasses. Our laughter was echoing throughout the whole building as we both were in hysterics. The lady attendant came in to see what we were doing, and when we explained that we were here for the books awards she joined in our fun and had her picture taken with the two crazy Canucks. Oh, the videos and photos we took that day! LOL

The next day, we headed off to the International Book Fair, situated out on the streets. There were blocks and blocks of books! Suddenly though, as I sauntered along the sidewalk, my left knee gave out on me! Oh, the pain! I held it, silently swearing like a trooper in the crowded streets. I guessed (correctly) that compensating by putting my weight on the left knee, due to the damaged right knee, had finally hit its end.

The only good thing about now having two bum knees is I had to fly home in first class for the extra legroom. Hmmm... a girl could get used to this!

When I arrived home, straight to the doctor I went and then in for an MRI on the right knee. Prognosis was "torn meniscus." I did not need to know the diagnosis on the left, as it was the exact same pain as the right. So here I was, hobbling around with both knees torn. Oh, the pain was exhausting! No longer could I ride my horse,

Hughie, and soon he came home from the stable. Now Hughie was actually happy with that as he loved living at our house instead of the barn. He had huge pastures to graze in, sunshine and freedom.

The following spring came and I was scheduled for knee surgery. The surgeon wanted to do each knee at separate times, but I refused: It was both knees, or nothing. I knew what I was like with hospitals and anesthesia in general, and my body just does not handle either very well.

On the morning of the surgery, the doctor came into the OR waiting room wearing big yellow rubber boots. As he explained the procedure for orthoscopic knee surgery, I couldn't help but ask him, "Why the boots?" He laughed and said, "When I am cutting inside your knees, we use water to help flush out the torn pieces of meniscus, and the tiny pieces of bone from the arthritis floating in there, to protect the remaining stable meniscus. I had to wear boots as the water splashes onto the floor." "Oh I see." I said.

Once the surgery was done, I arrived back in my hospital room, supposedly to be there for several more hours. The person in the bed beside me was moaning and groaning from their orthoscopic knee surgery, and I looked at Bud and said, "I am out of here: go find me a wheelchair!" Bud knew better than to argue with me on this point. I must have had that look in my eye that said, "There is no discussing this." Naturally, the bladder speaks up and says, "Hey, we need to go, now!" Therefore, I rang the buzzer for the nurse to tell her that I had to pee. It was now two hours from the time I went down to the OR and back into my room. The nurse came in and helped me to stand and I walked very slowly to the bathroom. (No vertigo: YEAH!) When I came out, I informed the nurse that I was leaving. "Are you sure?" she asked. "I have stood, I have walked and I have peed, so I am good" I replied. "We have never had anyone come in and go out within two hours. Everyone stays until the late afternoon." she said while shaking her head.

"I am not like most people" I replied. Just then, Bud came into the room with the wheelchair. "There is no reason for me to stay. My bed can be given to someone who needs it way more than I do." I said as I leaned on the bed for support and slowly swung my butt around and plopped into the chair. Then off we went down the hall, Bud pushing, me in in the wheelchair with both my legs sticking straight out in front of me, guiding me towards freedom.

On my two-week checkup, I enquired about when I could start riding again. The surgeon told me that riding was going to have to wait until my knees were fully healed, which was about one year, and I was NOT allowed to do any jumping. Now, that *jumping* part *was* going to be a bit of a problem, since Hughie stands 17'2 hh and I only dismount by jumping off. What to do, what to do? This would turn out to become one of the biggest factors in my future riding endeavours. In the meantime, Hughie was enjoying being at home with his buddy, Beasley, to keep him company while the mares in the other pasture were giving them the googly eyes.

#doubleornothing #recoverytime #torideornototride

Story 35

Mario Reborn, NOT!

It was May and we were off on the Alaskan Cruise with Marta and Don, friends of ours.

For years I had heard my Mom and Dad say that they were going to go to Alaska, maybe go on the boat tour. Sadly, Mom died and they never did go. Then Dad and Olive got together and they, too, decided that they wanted to go on the Alaskan cruise. Again, fate intervened, as Olive passed away before they could go.

I have heard it said many times that we teach our children things in life, but we just don't know what they are learning from us. What I learned from both Mom and Dad and Olive and Dad was: instead of saying what you want to do, _do it_! Life is short and none of us knows how long we have on this earth to live, so start living for today and set goals for tomorrow.

Our cruise ship had a racetrack on the top deck. We all decided on one of the days we were at sea that we would try our hand at racing the cars on the open deck. I had visions of me hurdling around a corner, missing it and flying off into the ocean! LOL! Race day came and as we were all sitting in our cars, waiting for the green light to come on, the announcer told us that when we enter the track, we must maintain a slow speed until one lap is completed, then off we could go. In addition, if we were getting into trouble, they could cut our engine, or if you were ramming other drivers, your engine would be cut. Ok, all clear I thought to myself.

I was sitting in the front car and was determined that I was going to remain there. Methinks I am a bit competitive: heck, I am competitive with myself in life! LOL

The green light flashed, off we went, doing the slow climb to the top of the track and weaving around the corners until the first lap was done. Bam! Off I shot, heading around the corners like Mario himself, holding back the others so that they could not pass easily. I was in my element, still leading after several laps. Yippee! As I approached the corner that goes past the pits, my car suddenly stopped running. I was frantically pumping the gas pedal but to no avail! Others were whipping past me as I limped down the hill and around the corner. What the heck was going on as I continued to try to get gas to my limp car? Suddenly, vroom! Off we went again, but now I was almost last in the race! As I sped around the corner, several cars were piled up and the yellow flag was waving at us to slow down. No passing allowed during this lap until the accident was cleared. Finally, we got the go ahead with the checkered flag and off I went again, trying to make up time and spaces with the other cars, weaving in and out trying to pass, but someone in front of me kept cutting me off. Grrrr! As I was about to pass this jerk, we got the checkered flag to go into the pits. The race was over.

I looked up at the score board to see that I had finished in sixth place. It was a great finish if there had indeed been more cars than six, and my car did not break down.

I realized later that the establishment (the racetrack crew) had cut the gas to my car! Seriously, what is wrong with you people? I had that race in the bag! I guess they wanted everyone to have the taste of being in the lead. I doubt that was it, but I will go with that instead of what I really think.

Then again, maybe the vision of me flying over the railing of the boat into the ocean was really a premonition…

#racingdemon #mario #cuttingmygas #adrenalinjunkie

Story 36

Splish, Splash and Flash

We were back in Mexico with the *Living Benefits Company*, and one of the sales advisors asked us if we were interested in renting a sailboat to sail to the island of Marietas. On Marietas, there was a hidden crater beach along with an animal and bird sanctuary. We could also do some snorkelling around the island while we were there. The boats were not allowed to land on the island but we could snorkel to it if we wanted. The island of Marietas is a crucial nesting, refuge, and breeding ground for 92-odd species of birds and hosts the largest breeding colonies of brown boobies, white-capped marine swallow, band-tailed swallow and the laughing seagull. Around the island are approximately 115 different species of fish, sharks and rays, including 10 mammal species like dolphins and whales. The coral reef hosts about 200 different other species, including 11 reptile species such as iguanas, lizards, rattlesnakes and sea and earth turtles. Also, protected in and around the island are 44 species of flora and fauna.

Our tour guide that day was Ricardo, a marine biologist who happens to own his own 10-person sailing boat. Now Ricardo is not what one would expect a Marine Biologist to look like; he had nearly waist-length light brown hair in dread locks, with a small beard sprouting from his chin. As we headed out in the bay, he chatted away about his life as a Marine Biologist and how he came to be in Mexico. Hours slowly slipped by as we sailed towards Marietas. Along the way, we were able to see many whales and dolphins.

I think I was born to be on the sea, for travelling on a boat was calming and soothing. Now I cannot say I have that same feeling about being *in* the water but I am game to trying almost anything. The last time I had come on a tour to Marietas I had a removable leg brace for my broken ankle and the tour company refused to let me off the boat. This time was going to be different!

Over this past year, I had been doing physiotherapy in the swimming pool to help strengthen my knees after double knee surgery. After each session, I would rinse the pool chlorine out my tankini bathing suit and had it ready for the next day or two.

Upon reaching Marietas, Ricardo asked who would like to go and visit the secluded beach and wildlife. Several of us, Bud and I included, raised our hands. As we lined up to leave the sailboat to climb aboard the motorboat, Ricardo handed us our life vests, which consisted of an orange wrap-around-your-waist thing. Once settled into the boat, off we went. As we approached the beach, the boat stopped and idled backwards, holding its position in the rough waters. Ricardo then proceeded to tell us that we now had to jump into the deep crashing waves, which were pounding the boat and crashing on to the shore! I looked at him then looked over the side of the boat at the deep waves and rocks below and said, "Are you nuts?" Here I was, sitting on the rocking boat with my clothes on since there was no place on the tiny sailboat to change into my bathing- suit bottoms. Thankfully, I had had the foresight to wear my swimming top under my shirt!

As he was bobbing in the water, looking up at me with a daring smile I might add, I stared back and said, "You bloody well better not let me drown!"

With a grin, he said, "No senorita I will not let you drown."

Reassured, I climbed up and lifted my legs over the side of the rocking boat. With a heave, I lifted myself up and over, headfirst into the rolling waves. I must say that it was not a graceful landing, and as the waves bashed me around, I was flaying to right myself and to surface. Finally, after what seemed like an eternity, I surfaced, spitting and coughing. Ricardo, true almost to his word, was there and helped me towards the shore. About ten feet away from the shore, where I could stand in the crashing waves, he left me to go help another. Not truly caring that I looked like a very ungraceful lump, I steadied myself from the excursion. Finally, not wanting to look like an absolute wimp, I gathered my strength, stood up and walked forward towards the arched entrance to the beach. My Capri sweat pants by this time felt like a hundred pounds, and were now full-length pants that kept wrapping themselves around both legs, impeding my not-so graceful walk to the beach area.

Whew: I made it to the crater beach! It is breathtaking, watching the waves roll in and sweep over the rocks, so much different than on the other side of the island we had entered on.

Too soon, it was time to leave. I was not looking forward to entering the ocean again but knew in order to get to the boat I was going to have to swim there. Not being a fan of deep water, especially with me in it, I looked at Ricardo and asked him, "So, how are we supposed to get back into the motorboat?'

With a twinkle in his eye he said, "Oh Senorita you will use the ladder!'

I looked at him in disbelief and said, "You have a ladder for the boat?"

Grinning at me, he nodded his head up and down. Right then and there I wanted to smack him! However, before I could he grabbed my hand and off into the crashing waves we went, him swimming like an otter and me like a drowning wildebeest, trying with all my might to do the dog paddle towards safety of the rocking boat! Once we arrived at the boat, Ricardo indicated for me to climb up the narrow ladder while he swam back to help others. When everyone was aboard, we headed back to the sailboat to have a drink and eat the lunch that was going to be served. As the crew was below deck getting the sandwiches ready I took the opportunity to wrap the towel around me and proceeded to peel off my soaked sweat pants and to put on my swimming suit bottoms, as snorkelling was next on the agenda.

With lunch over and chatting-time done, Ricardo asked who was ready to go snorkelling. All of our friends that bragged about going snorkelling when we were deciding which excursion to take, did not raise their hands.

Ricardo was standing there and said, "Surely someone must want to go?"

I thought about it for maybe a minute before I stood up and said that I would go. So, another couple that apparently did lots of snorkelling and I headed towards the side of the sailboat that we would be leaving from.

As I was making my way along, I looked back at our friends, shaking my head laughing and said, "You bunch of lily livered shits!"

Once again I found myself sitting on the side of the sailboat, looking at the deep water about four feet below me and wondered to myself, "What in the hell am I doing?"

The other two snorkelers had already jumped into the ocean and were swimming away, enjoying the pleasures of the deep blue.

Ricardo was bobbing up and down in the water, waving at me; it was time to join him. I was not so sure about this and was almost ready to refuse when the rest of the passengers started to chant my name. "Brenda! Brenda! Brenda!" Once again, I looked at all of them and said sarcastically, "You Shits."

With a big breath, I closed my eyes and pushed mysel off, landing eet first into the ocean. Once again I came up spitting and spurting. Ricardo was laughing and handed me a line that was attached to his vest. After adjusting my snorkel mask, he told me to hang on to the line that was attached to him for safety. I guess he did not want to lose one of his passengers to the murky deep ocean. I know I certainly did not want to get lost. Off we went, swimming towards the rocky cliffs that soared above and below the ocean.

What a beautiul sight to behold, the multicolored fish swimming below us, not seeming to be bothered by the turbulent water.

There were so many fish to see, when Ricardo wanted me to see a particular fish he would signal to me and point to the fish. As the waves crashed around us he made sure that I was not swimming too close to the rocky cliff beside us as we wandered around, swimming amongst the fish. As we swam over and around the coral ree there were sea turtles, parrot fish and I thought I had even seen a stingray. After a while, we came into a small bay where Ricardo indicated for me to take off my snorkel mask. As we treaded water, he showed me the brown boobies, explaining that this was their breeding season as we watched the mating dance that was going on above us. It was a very interesting conversation as we treaded water, bobbing up and down with the waves, chatting about the flora and auna that inhabited the island. As we bobbed in the water he pointed out the lizards and iguanas that were sunning themselves along the rocky out cliffs. He talked about things he had seen in his lie and I chatted about similar things in my life and the animals that surround us where we lived. We laughed about events that had happened to us in life. Little did I know I was probably going to be one of those events or memories that he will not soon forget!

As we continued swimming out of the enclosed bay, the waves were pushing me closer to Ricardo and without realizing it I was practically on top of him and my hand holding the tethering line was rubbing against his groin area. When I realized where my hand was, I quickly tried to move away but the ocean water was not having any of it and once again, here I was now rubbing along his body. "Oh my god" was all I could think of.

Ricardo, to his credit never looked at me, nor did he swim away to put some distance between us. I thought to myself, "Maybe he did not notice!" Relie flooded through me, thinking this wondrous thought.

Finally, and not a moment too soon, I might add, it was time to swim back to the boat. I had lifted up my snorkel mask so that I could get a better the view of the sailboat in the distance. As we slowly approached the sailboat I asked him, "How are we going to get up there?"

He looked at me, smiled that alarmingly seductive smile and simply replied, "Why I will boost you up from your behind." With his hand he indicated exactly how he would achieve this. The look on my face must have been priceless.

As he laughed, I looked back at him and said, "Not bloody likely." I don't think I could have been more embarrassed as I soon realized that Ricardo did in fact know where my hand had floated to.

Now don't get me wrong; Ricardo is a very likable fellow and there was no way a person could actually be mad at him. I know I certainly could not, but then again I was not willing to let him know that. I think that I failed at that attempt! LOL

Once we were closer to the sail boat I could not see how I was going to get back on it. I looked at him in disbelief: was he truly serious? His laughter rolled over the waves as he watched the look of horror cross my face.

All I could think was there was no way on God's green earth was he:

1. going to be able to lift me out of the water,
2. going to put his hand under my butt and push me up the four-foot side of his sailboat!

Possibly a shark would come and eat me before I managed to crawl and drag myself up and over the side of the boat! The sudden thought of a shark was very sobering since they did live in and around the island!

Ricardo, still smiling to himself, motioned for me to swim with him to the back of the sailboat where miraculously, a ladder was hanging! I turned to him and said as sarcastically as I could, "Why on earth did you make me jump in the dam water if you had a ladder?" Once again he was laughing. I thought to myself, "What a sod."

As I was attempting to climb the ladder and pull myself out of the water, the unthinkable happened! Remember when I said that I worked out in the swimming pool doing physiotherapy for the past year? Well apparently chloride can do things to your bathing suit, so with the combination of sea water, your bathing suit starts to, let's say, fall apart!

Just picture this: So here I am, Ricardo is right behind me, hanging on to the ladder as I am pulling myself out of the ocean and sadly the bottoms of my bathing suit were not willing to follow me out of the water and decided that they wished to remain behind!

As I felt my bottoms slip away, I quickly tried to grab ahold of them while being whipped back and forth on the ladder due to the waves crashing against the hull. Ricardo is laughing once again and I think the laughing seagulls were also enjoying the show that was happening.

To say that he got a full view of what God gave me would be an understatement, to say the least!

As I struggled to keep my bottoms on while trying to climb the ladder, I did not realize that my top had also decided that it preferred to follow the bottoms and had started to stretch down past the waist-level life-vest I was wearing! The only redeeming feature was that the life vest stopped my top from leaving altogether. As I leaned over the back of the boat, trying to get up, everyone, and I *mean everyone* was enjoying the full-breasted view! I did not realize this was happening until I was looking at pictures Bud, had taken while I was emerging out of the depths of hell to get into the boat.

Finally aboard, I staggered to the front of the boat with a towel wrapped around me, and while the crew was distracted with pulling the anchor and setting sail, I put my clothes on over my swim suit. As I sat there, I pulled my tank top on over the offending bathing suit top. Then I was able to peel off the remaining parts by pulling each shoulder strap down each arm, removing my arm from the straps, then pulling the rest down over my butt and down my legs. Next, with the towel wrapped around my waist, I removed my bottoms one leg at a time and slid them off. Then, I quickly pulled on my wet stretched, out-of-shape sweat-pants. I felt it was better to have my wet pants on to sit comfortably on the way back, knowing that they were not able to leave my body any time soon!

As we ventured back to Puerto Vallarta, we were escorted by a pod of dolphins, whales and a laughing Ricardo who kept looking at me and winking.

Oh God.

My bathing suit never left Mexico, I might add!

#laughteristhebestmedicine #timeforanewswimmingsuit #birthdaysuit #flasherornot

Myself and Ricardo after entering the water

Story 37

Seriously!

As many of you know by now, I am NOT a fan of water; I swim like a rock despite many attempts at swimming lessons. The horizontal position in the water eludes me!

Therefore, when we were visiting Bud's sister Nancy and her husband Scott at their cabin on Black Donald Lake in Ottawa this fall, they suggested that we should go tubing. The boat was still in the water and the chair tube was ready to use one last time before everything was stored away for the winter. Now, I am game for just about anything, so with assurance that we would not end up in the water, I agreed to go for a spin.

Nancy came out with her swimsuit on, and since I did not bring one, I just had on my usual clothes. I was not thinking of using a life preserver, since I was not going in the water, but decided "better safe than sorry." Therefore, with a sippy cup of wine in my hand and my phone camera in my shirt just under the life vest, I climbed aboard the floating chair with Nancy.

Three could sit on the chair, so Nancy was on one side and I on the other. All was going well, we were laughing and sipping wine. As the boat started to leave the dock, the rope was not tight and the chair was a bit tippy. I thought maybe I was unbalancing it so I moved over closer to Nancy. Ok, wrong thing to do and the floating chair tube leaned over towards the water. I quickly climbed back to the side I had been sitting on. We were slowly floating out into the lake, the rope was still not tight enough and the chair tube was leaning really far back, so to help counter that, I was leaning forward.

Meanwhile, Nancy was waving at Bud, the spotter, and Scott, the driver to get going so that the tow rope would tighten, but they apparently were not getting the message because all of a sudden over backwards we both went into the water.

I was glad to have that life vest on as I came up, spitting and coughing! Nancy, on the other hand, was laughing, and soon she had me laughing too as we treaded water. Trying to get to the back of the boat to climb back on that miserable chair was a feat since the boat was quite the distance away from us. Here I was, holding the wine glass over the water, and I had quickly grabbed my phone out of my shirt before it became extremely wet. Nancy took my phone in her hand and started to swim towards the back of the boat, outdistancing me as I dog-paddled with one arm in the same direction. Finally, I made it to the back of the boat. Now the next step was to attempt to climb up the ladder on the back of the boat with the inboard motor running. All I could think of was my toes being shredded off with the blades. Hence, the act that this boat had an "inboard motor" did not enter my thoughts! Now bear in mind, I had had two knee surgeries the previous year, and I am not what you would call dainty or tiny. I am a full-figured woman, so hauling myself up that skinny ladder wearing soaking wet clothes and a life vest was not an easy feat! However, I refused to be daunted in the task, so grunting and groaning silently, I pulled myself up that ladder. The only good thing was I did not fart in the excursion, thank god.

Finally up, I now had to get back onto that damn floating chair, which again was threatening to flip over! With Nancy and I saely aboard, we told the boys to *"hit it!"* so that the rope would pull the front of the tube down. Well, the boys were not thinking that we should go that fast, so here Nancy and I were, skipping along the water with our hair dangling in the waves behind us. Try as we might, we could not get the guys to go faster: the hand signals were not working! At last, they got the message and gunned it! The tube ew forward, and for a brief minute, thinking that I was going to fly over the handlebars, I was terrified for my life! Nancy, in the meantime, was sipping her wine and laughing! As we careened along, I looked over the side and saw the huge wave below me that was about four feet deep. As I stared at this huge hole of water I thought, "Holy shit, if this tube slips one inch, we are going end-over-end into that trough of water, never to be seen again!" Now I was leaning towards the centre of the tube, hanging on for dear life!

Scott took the corner to go back towards the cabin. As he was turning the speed- boat in the half circle, the tube *shot* out to the side like a rocket! I think everyone in Alberta and the surrounding area heard my blood-curdling scream as the tube rocketed towards the front of the boat, only to be whipped back into place behind the boat once more as it sped past us. As we careened back into place, we were hitting waves from the wake of the boat and flying through the air! Both Nancy and I were air borne as the tube jetted in and over the waves, my death-defying screams echoing off the shores as we whipped around the lake at break-neck speed! Nancy, in the meantime, was still laughing! Several more rounds we went, and soon the terror was gone, replaced with exhilaration! There were plenty more blood curdling screams from me as we hit the deep trough of water running alongside the tube. The tube shot out of the water like a bullet, as we hung on, our legs were bouncing up so high they were almost smacking us in the face! Wow what a ride!

Soon it was time to taxi back to our starting spot. Once more, the minute the rope was slack, the chair tube flipped over and Nancy and I ended up back into the lake! This time, instead of trying to climb into the boat we would swim back to the boat launch. When we finally got the tube flipped back up the right way, we threw our wine cups into the seat and started to head for the dock, Nancy dragging the tube while I pushed from behind. Finally, we made it back to the dock where there was a ladder to aid our climb out of the water.

Everyone was laughing about the flipping tube, which, by the way, had never ever flipped over once *all summer* with any of the other riders! (Makes me wonder, hmmm.)

Maybe one day I will conquer the water, but then again maybe not.

#wipingatbreakneckspeed #adrenalinjunkie #lifevestssaveslives #blackdonaldlake #familytime

Story 38

Are you my Human?

The day Oliver came...Bud is not a cat person so if we were going to acquire another cat it would have to be a very unique and different cat.

We did have a calico cat that was edging near 16 years old. I would not say that Katt was a people cat, she was very particular on who she decided she liked or disliked. If she liked you then she would allow you to pet her and she would allow you to share in her shedding hair. Which was considerable.

Katt came into our lives one Christmas when we went to visit my daughter and her husband. It was about a five-hour drive one way trip, so no thought had entered our minds that we would be travelling home with another animal. At the time we had a small black Tibetan Spanish / Maltese Shih Tzu cross puppy named Ty who was about 6 months old. He was the cutest little guy with devil ears and also the most stubborn in his dietary likes and dislikes. This trait would carry on for his whole life, his attitude was I do not do tricks for food and I don't eat dog food. Period.

We had just lost Ty about 6 months prior and Katt was not long for the world, neither of us was looking to get another pet.

Tukker, Ty's nephew was feeling the absence of Ty and moped around the house. He had become sad and lonely, whining and fussing at the time. Now Tukker had never been needy, but he was soon becoming a bit of a handful because of our work schedule. He wanted to be with us where ever we went and we felt so bad for him that we started to take him everywhere.

It was late fall, and one day this feral black cat arrived on our doorstep, Bud let Tukker out to go pee, Tukker spied the strange cat and the hot chase was on. Tukker's corkscrew tail was twirling like a baton guiding him in his race across the yard, it acted like a rudder on a boat, spinning his tail one way to turn and the other way to rebound. This went on for weeks. Finally Tukker has something to do and his disposition started to change. Now Tukker is not much bigger than Ty and this black cat was bigger than him, but that did not bother Tukker. As days went by the black cat soon figured out that Tukker, was all bark and chase but no bite.

After this realization, the black cat started to follow me around the yard, tripping me as I walked, jumping on the horses backs as I fed them or weaving between their legs as I sorted out the hay. It became so bad that when I had to move the tractor, the black cat was there laying under the big tractor wheels or just sitting there in the way, refusing to move. I was afraid I was going to run him over so I decided that he would have to starting riding on the tractor with me, or else he was going to become a black splat under the tractor tire. The black cat was not so sure about the first time. I was certainly worried about this feral cat clawing and ripping at me to let him go, but after a conversation on the dos and don'ts of tractor riding he settled down. Not so dumb this cat.

When I would move the big round bales, the black cat would suddenly jump on top and go for a wild ride as I took the bales into the corrals to feed. I watched him like a hawk to make sure that he didn't decide to jump off and I run him over. He was worse than having little kids around the moving equipment, at least with kids I could yell at them to get back, but not this cat. Oh no, he was determined that he was going where ever I was and that was that.

I knew that if this cat was going to stay, and apparently he was, then he needed a name. Many names came forward, one in particular was Denis the Menace. But nothing seemed to suit his personality and certain not a name he liked. Then one day as Bud and I were driving to town, Bud said maybe Oliver or Oscar.

So to say that Oliver had to win over Bud's heart was a near impossible feat, but he had for Bud to even consider giving him a name.

Score one for Oliver.

Oliver decided that cold winter weather was coming and maybe I should be in that house these humans keep going into. So one day Oliver decided to take the chance and ran into the house the minute

I opened to door to go in. This was not part of my plan for Oliver and I tried to catch him to put him back outside but he was wily. I could read his mind, hmm nice digs and warm too, I think I will stay. Suddenly Tukker came around the corner, seeing this interloper and intruder Tukker put on the chase. Oliver was shocked to see that white fur ball again giving chase, fluffed up his body to scare the dog, but to no avail that white demon kept coming. Luckily, I was still standing by the door when Oliver and Tukker rounded the corner into the porch in a headlong pursuit. I simply opened the door and Oliver went flying out, Tukker screeching to a halt at the open door. With much satisfaction on his face, Tukker turned around and trotted back into the house, while Oliver sat on the sidewalk contemplating his next move.

Oliver continued to try to get into the house, and I knew that when the weather turned colder I would have a dilemma on my hands. So I went into our storage shed found the old litter box and some litter and set it up in the barn. Next I called Oliver and took him to the barn in the vain hopes of teaching a 1.5 yr. old feral cat how to use the litter. Upon setting Oliver in the litter box and showing him how to dig, he looked at me with disgust, hopped out and shook his paws to remove the little bits of litter stuck in them and sauntered off. This was not going well.

So I decided to leave the litter box in the barn in hopes that Oliver when he was in there when I was feeding the horses that he might start to use it. That was wishful thinking on my part, for Oliver certainly had a different plan in mind and it did not included living in the barn like an animal.

After we had put Katt to sleep, due to a cancerous tumor on her face, Oliver decided that the house was his main goal. With Katt now gone he did not have an obstacle in his path, so the games began in earnest. He had to figure out how he was going to get in and stay in the house and his mission was just that.

Within days of the passing of Katt, Oliver once more managed to get into the house, this time there was the Mexican standoff between him and Tukker, the stare down, who will blink first. Neither of them were moving, just standing there staring at each other. Suddenly Oliver decided to throw Tukker off his game and sauntered over to him, rubbing and purring. I guess showing him the love. Tukker was a bit disgusted with this and turned and walked away.

Score two for Oliver.

As I looked at Oliver relishing in his conquest thoughts were running through my mind: now I have a male feral un-litter trained cat in my house. Now what?

Most people would say just kick him outside, but there was something about Oliver that both Bud and I could feel. Oliver was here at our house for a reason.

So, with Oliver enjoying his victory, I headed off out to the barn to get the dreaded litter box. If Oliver was staying in the house, he was going to have to know the ground rules.

I set the litter box in the bathroom by our back door, then proceeded to gather up Oliver and have a serious conversation with him. That included this is where you go to the bathroom and if you mess or spray in the house you are out the door, no scratching the furniture, no getting on the counters, you can chase and get the mice if there are any and while outside NO eating the little birds. I explained that if he was going to stay here this is what the rules were. I left out the fact that he was going to have to be vaccinated and neutered. I thought I would save that for another day or maybe not at all. If Oliver decided to stay living at our house then these two things were going to happen. So I gave Oliver one month to decide to stay or go back to wherever he came from.

So he stayed, score three for Oliver.

It has now the turning of spring and Oliver has made himself quite at home, he is a drooler, loves his cuddling with me, playing in the toilet bowl, killed my printer by sticking his paws in to grab the paper shooting out, has been on the roof of almost every building. He even managed to get on the hay shed roof where he was stuck yowling his fool head off. Rescue me, mom.

So far Oliver has abided by all the ground rules that were laid down. During this time a bond started to form between him and Tukker, I can't say that it is love but Oliver continues to try to play with Tukker and Tukker continues to ignore him. But it is all an act on Tukker's part, for when Oliver is outside chasing the mice Tukker is watching for him to come to the house. At night time if Oliver is outside Tukker makes a fuss until I go to the door to call Oliver to come in. And by the way, Oliver comes to his name when I call. LOL

Score four for Oliver and his new home.

Frankly I am not sure how Oliver came to be, at times it feels like he dropped out of the sky just for us.

#rescuepet #who-rescued-who #blackcats

Story #39

Exercise is overrated, if you almost die doing it!

It was a cold and miserable winter so far; the kind that refuses to let you go outside for fear of having your face frozen in place, then to shatter in a million pieces if you so much as sneezed!

It was the kind of cold that seeps into your bones and will not let go.

As winter usually goes, it helps to add extra weight to your body, you know that insulating fat we get when we are not moving around much. That fat that comes and sits with you on the couch as you watch reruns of anything and everything since the new programs are not scheduled yet. That no man's land, where time stops, and we slowly cease inhaling life.

Well, I decided that enough was enough! I needed to get outside and move more than what my normal chore routine was with our horses.

They do say that walking helps to lose weight, so I decided that walking was it. Our driveway is half a mile long, so that would be a good start I figured. Then I had another great idea, I had extra square hay bales left over from a few years back that were stacked in my hay shed, taking up valuable room from the round bales that I was using.

My horses certainly did not need the extra hay judging by their weight, but maybe the neighbor's horses would enjoy them The Alfalfa hay has high in protein and instead of throwing it away I figured I would give it to the neighbor's horses that were pawing through the snow for food. Every time we came home, the neighbor's horses were standing at their fence looking at us as we drove and turned up our driveway. For the past month I swear I could hear them talking to me yelling: 'Hey, stop feed us we are hungry. We know you can hear us.'

Therefore, with the new calf sled (a sled for hauling newborn calves) I bought at Peavey mart, I decided that it would be great to haul a square hay bale down the driveway and into the field along their fence line to feed those horses. Now, how hard can that be? I did not want to just walk into their yard, so I figured that feeding them along the fence would be better than trespassing. In doing this I thought maybe they would stop yelling at me, if not then I was going crazy.

Going the first half-mile was not bad. Our west- running driveway sloped down, so thinking that I was still in my youth, I was able to ride on the sled with the bale every few feet. Running and jumping on a moving sled is not as easy when you are over 60! For some reason, I thought it would be easier! Bruised knees and skinned shins later, I arrived at the bottom of our driveway. Next was the short 50 yards trek down the road, down into the ditch of snow and up the other side to the neighbor's field with my hay bale in tow. So far so good, but soon I was panting for air. Cold air was being sucked into my warm lungs, freezing everything in its path! The hard-crusted, snow was up to my knees and I still had to go at least a 1/8 of a mile! Slowly but surely, I forged my way through the snow to a place where I could drop-off the bale of hay. With sweat running off my face and gasping for air, I finally made it, dreading the thought of having to slog my way back. However, I was here now.

As I threw the pieces of bale over the fence, there was not a horse in sight. They had watched me coming down our driveway, neighing as I came, but when I turned the corner to go down the road to the opposite side of the fence, they did not figure that part out. You could almost hear them saying, "What? Where are you going?" So, after distributing the hay evenly all over the area, I waited. After a few minutes, I decided to give it a chance and called for them. Since these were not my horses, I wasn't sure if they would come to someone's call. My only experience with them was when they raced across our field, after their great escape from their own field, running at full speed as if the devil was on their tails, and certainly not stopping when their owner called them!

Well, it did not take long for them to figure out where I was and they came running through the trees, knee-deep in the snow. I stood there thinking how dam easy that was for them until I saw the sheep coming, dragging its wool across the snow, trying to step in the footprints of the horses. I felt just like that sheep, dragging my carcass through the deep snow.

After a bit of a break, it was time to turn around and go back the way I came. I thought foolishly to myself, "Well, this should be easier, since I already broke trail." NOT

Once again, I was wheezing like a chain smoker, sucking on the last bits of a last cigarette. (I know what that sounds like, since my ex-mother-in-law was a heavy chain-smoking fiend.) Then, to help matters, my asthma decided that it was a good time to kick in. There were moments in that struggle to get back to the road that I thought I was dying. Then there were moments that I wished I did. I was exhausted and sweating like a sumo wrestler, minus the thong thing they wear. Luckily for me, I have a husband who (probably has a bit more sense than me while I am in my 'Wonder Woman thinking mode") had brought down the gator (fancy ATV) and parked it on the road, waiting for me.

I must say it took a bit to get there, but I did it!

The horses were happily eating the hay, and here I was, riding back in the gator to a warm cozy house, thinking smugly to myself, 'I must have lost at least five pounds with that excursion!"

Sometimes, no matter what you do, things just do not work out the way you planned!

#weightinyoursixties #hatescales #clothesshrinkinthewinter #happyhorses #ishouldbuyathreadmill #horseschatting

Story 40

No good deed goes unpunished!

Bud has a favorite saying, "No good deed goes unpunished." We once watched a documentary on Garth Brooks, who said something very similar: "It is a blessing and a curse". After this day I really understood that phrase.

Winter was setting in and we were heading into another cold snap. January weather was showing us who was in control, and it certainly was *not* us! We had had a heavy snowfall during the night with strong winds whipping the snow into huge drifts along the tree line of our driveway. For the past few days, I had moved some of our extra square bales down to the neighbors' horses. Our horses certainly did not need the hay as they were plump pumpkins already. Looking out the window at the freezing weather, I figured that today, as I plowed our driveway, I would haul a few square bales in the front-end loader and deliver them to the neighbor's horses and sheep again. I was not going to make the mistake of tackling the deep snow with my calf sled loaded with hay, a lesson learned just the other day!

So I bundled up, looking like Nanook of the North and headed west, down our half-mile long driveway, with the rear blade plowing the snow and a front bucket full of hay. As I came down our driveway, the neighbor's horses watched me. They knew what was coming and were whinnying in delight until I turned north out of our driveway and headed down the main road, away from them. I could almost hear them say, "Hey, wait where are you going?" It was bitterly cold and my ski goggles were starting to frost up by the time I reached the next approach, another ½ mile away. I then turned into the other neighbor's field that led back south alongside the main road, towards the field where the horses were. Snow was over four feet deep in spots, and as the wheels of the tractor plowed through the drifts, snow blew up into my face. I had the back blade lifted as high as it could go, but as I moved through the drifts the blade was ploughing snow around behind me, and it was whirling up along the back of my jacket. Brrrr: I didn't think that ½ mile trek would ever end! Literally *covered* from head to toe in snow, I was starting to look like a white Sasquatch with my yellow goggles and my toque sticking up in a point to cover my ponytail! Add the huge triple-layer of thermal underwear, ski pants and many coats, bundled up I was now probably ten times my usual size! Yes, I definitely looked like the Yeti!

Finally, I reached the our neighbor's west-running fence line and turned the tractor to follow it down another ¼ mile to where I had thrown the hay over the other day. When I reached the right spot, I put the tractor in 'Park' and climbed down. I jumped down and landed in snow that was up to my thighs! There I was, stuck in the snow. I must have looked like the Michelin Man, rolling around in the deep snow, trying to get up. I had visions of the local newspaper headline featuring the spring cover story: Frozen wife of the Michelin Man found.

Did you know that deep, thick, heavy snow is like quicksand; the more you struggle to get out of it, the further down you go? Mind you, I have never been in quicksand but I am assuming, from books I read, that it is the same experience, minus the suffocating sand pouring into all your pores in your head. I suppose the snow would do the same thing if given a chance, but not today for this girl. I had a mission to complete!

After considerable effort, lots of grunts, groans and sweat, I managed to get unstuck and slogged my way through the thigh-high snow alongside the tractor, working my way to the front bucket where the hay was so I could cut the strings on the bales. By the time I finally managed to get all the strings cut, the horses still had not figured out where I had gone! I chuckled to myself, figuring that they were a bit peeved that I was not there with the green golden gift from the gods. As I plowed my way through the deep drifts along the fence line, I could not help but think, "Boy, they'd better appreciate this!" Deep down I knew they would, and it gave me satisfaction to realize that they would be munching on the Gift from the Gods soon. I slowly moved back and forth from the tractor to the fence, throwing the hay over, making several piles so that everyone got their fair share. When I was done, I hollered,

'Come on.' It did not take long for the horses to find me, plowing their way through the deep snow, weaving once again in and out of the trees. Even the sheep made it as she climbed and clawed her way, following the deep tracks the horses made. Everyone settled down to the buffet of luscious green hay piles laid out for them.

Once I was sure that everyone was eating, I struggled back to the tractor. Putting my foot on the bottom step, I heaved myself out of the snow and climbed up to the seat. As I was putting back on all my mittens I realized that one was missing. I had had to peel it off in order to get the knife out of my jacket pocket to cut the strings. As I scanned around the tractor from my seat perch, I spied it lying nearly under the back wheel of the tractor on the opposite side, where the snow was equally as deep. Down I got once more and struggled now to the back of the tractor, heaving myself up on the back blade to reach for the missing mitten. Now here I was, teetering over the back blade, reaching as far as I could, hoping that I was not about to go head first into the snow! Thankfully I was able to extract myself backwards once I had the tip of the mitten in between my now numb fingers.

With frozen fingers and toes, I put the tractor in gear and turned it around, spinning in the deep snow. It bucked like a young stallion as it tried to gain a foothold in the deep snow to move forward. Meanwhile, I was speaking to the tractor like she understands me, encouraging her to bite the ground and move forward. Finally, the wheels grabbed grass that was lying under the snow and we propelled forward to return along the track we had made earlier.

Today, as I was heading back home, the two previously mentioned phrases came to mind: the horses were blessed with hay on a very cold day and I was cursed with freezing in the act of feeding them. LOL, no good deed goes unpunished, but I would do it again if need be. Maybe one day I will get a tractor with a cab. Here's to dreaming!

I will put that on my wish list when the economy turns around, if I do not freeze to death before I get back to the house and a warm fireplace!

#Michelinman #freezingweather #nogooddeedgoesunpunished #ablessingandacurse

About the Author

A Woman with a Purpose – Brenda Hammon

Brenda Hammon is an Alberta based philanthropist, entrepreneur, Intuitive and Psychic Medium, international best-selling author, goal setter and big dreamer with a mission in life to create positive change for women and end abuse. She is an award-winning author of 5 books, an International speaker, and a vocal advocate for helping people overcome traumatic pasts. Brenda fully believes that when we share our stories and stand together, we can change the world to be a better place for all.

When Brenda sets a goal, she is unstoppable, even if she has to start from scratch. In years past she bred, raised and trained her own horses and achieved a prestigious 3rd place standing in the highly competitive Canadian Nationals Dressage Circuit. In 2004 Brenda became a fulltime entrepreneur and over the next 13 years she built companies that fulfilled her passion for helping others achieve their dreams. After ending her 21year dysfunctional marriage, Brenda dove into the life insurance business where she found one of her true passions in helping others in times of trouble. Brenda continues to be a top, trusted insurance advisor and CEO of Spirit Creek Group Inc. and CEO of Spirit Creek Financial.

Brenda has published 5 books, 3 of which were International Best Sellers, all are Canadian Best Sellers and 1 an International Reader's Favorites award winner. She published her first book in 2015 revealing the deep dark secrets of her past and what she had to do to replace her old life with the life she knew she was truly meant to live. Brenda now speaks on stages telling her story and helping others to find their own voices and to live the life of their dreams. She is passionate about breaking the cycle of silence! She not only courageously writes about her own story, but also gives other women and men a voice by compiling and publishing their stories. To that end, she launched Sacred Hearts Rising, which is an anthology Series, a compilation of stories from women and men who have overcome seemingly insurmountable odds, and also, an event by the same name which honors and inspires people to lead a better life.

The first compilation, Sacred Hearts Rising: Breaking the Silence One Story at a Time, launched March 2018 and was an instant International Best Seller, the second compilation Sacred Hears Rising: Finding Your Wing: launched in March 2019 and also became an overnight Best Seller.

Seeing the need for more people to speak their truths, Brenda created the Sacred Hearts Rising Summit: It's Time, an annual event, which honors our stories and inspires women and men to lead a better way of life.

Brenda's goal is to reach out to every woman and man, to let them know they are not alone, and that change is possible.

Brenda is seriously committed to giving back to the community. She has raised funds by jumping out of a plane for a women's shelter and has raised funds to help an International Orphanage in Mexico and local organizations who are struggling to keep help helping those in need. Every year Brenda and her family help raise the spirits of 45 seniors at Christmas when they donate gift bags to two Senior Complex's in her community.

Brenda's two mottos are "how hard can it be?" and 'go big or go home" and she lives her life to the fullest.

You can connect with Brenda via:

Web: www.brendahammon.com www.sacredheartsrising.com
Facebook: facebook.com/brenda.hammon.9
Twitter: @HammonBrenda
Instagram: BrendaHammon
LinkedIn: Brenda(Bud Portwood)Hammon

www.ingramcontent.com/pod-product-compliance
Lightning Source LLC
Chambersburg PA
CBHW071412070526
44578CB00003B/562